Teach Yourself Guitar

Harry Taussig

Oak Publications, New York
Music Sales Limited, London

Book Design by Jean Hammons

©1971 Oak Publications
33 West 60th Street
New York, New York 10023

Music Sales Limited
78 Newman Street
London, W.1

Quick Fox Limited
40 Nugget Avenue, Agincourt, Ontario, Canada

Music Sales (Pty.) Limited
27 Clarendon Street, Artarmon, Sydney, NSW, Australia

Library of Congress Card Catalogue #: 70-93959
International Standard Book # 0-8256-0010-3

Contents

Acknowledgements

I would like to thank the many people, both my teachers and students, who have helped this book come about either directly or indirectly. Space severely limits the number of people I can mention so I must restrict myself to those who physically contributed to this book. To those who contributed spiritually my thanks en masse. My sincerest thanks go to Don Garwood and John Ruggiero for assistance in annotation of Carter Family material, to Bob Steenson for arranging Fennario in Open C tuning, to David Cohen, Bernard Pearl, Mike Birnbaum and David Polacheck for helpful discussions regarding the music, to John Upton for aid in organizing the teaching format, to Jon Lundberg for discussions of musical styles and keeping me in fine guitars, and again to Don Garwood for invaluable aid with the chapter on Monotonic Bass and the many fruitful and probing discussions of just about everything concerning guitar. And Sioux, for editorial assistance, patience, tolerance, and love.

Harry Taussig

Preface

Many may view this book as a second edition of *Instrumental Techniques of American Folk Guitar.* The same general organization has been used, many of the same songs appear, and the use of Carter style as an introduction to fingerpicking has been retained. On the other hand, *Teach Yourself Guitar* is for the beginner and *Instrumental Techniques of American Folk Guitar* was for the intermediate or advanced student. Many more songs and musical examples are used in this book to provide a slower progression in difficulty between the songs, thus making learning easier. A careful comparison of this book and *Instrumental Techniques of American Folk Guitar* will disclose the fact that very few of the songs used in that book have been used directly here. Most of the songs have been rearranged and edited to suit the purpose of instruction further than in the first book.

The student who wishes a quick, fast-paced introduction to the styles of American folk guitar will want to use *Instrumental Techniques of American Folk Guitar.* If, however, the student wishes a more thorough, a more detailed and smoother instruction book the current book, *Teach Yourself Guitar,* was written for him. A section is provided at the end in which the student may arrange his own guitar solos.

A Note To Teachers

This book is well suited for either group or private instruction in folk guitar. The lessons are graded and can be assigned as the teacher sees fit. For the rapidly advancing student some of the material can be omitted since it is designed to provide practice in a specific point by giving several musical examples for one point. For slower students the teacher should be provided with sufficient material in this book, or he can easily supplement the lesson plans presented here with his own material. In any teaching situation, it is highly recommended that the questions (which are an elementary form of programmed learning) be retained.

Any comments or suggestions for revision of this book, either by inclusion or by ommission, would be greatly appreciated by the author.

Important
Read This First

This book is intended to provide the beginning guitar student the necessary background of instruction and experience required for the detailed study of traditional American guitar styles. We will mainly be concerned with developing instrumental styles and skills. Thus we will be learning how to play solos on the guitar and the accompaniment of vocal parts will be used only in the introductory chapter. This will enable the student, who wants to play guitar but cannot or does not wish to sing, to concentrate on developing guitar skills. For accompaniment techniques, other books can be consulted concurrently (i.e., *The Folksingers Guitar Guide* by Jerry Silverman, Oak.).

In this book you will find instruction, songs, examples and exercises leading up to the skills necessary to study the guitar playing of Mississippi John Hurt, Mance Lipscomb, Rev. Gary Davis, Merle Travis, the Carter Family and many others. The musical examples used in this book have been devised to provide practice in a specific function; they should not be considered "accurate" notations of the playing of the artists associated with the particular songs. Accurate notations should be studied to build a repertoire only after appropriate skills have been acquired. These accurate notations are available elsewhere (*Masters of Instrumental Blues Guitar* by Don Garwood, *Country Blues Guitar* by Stephen Grossman, *American Fingerpicking Styles* by Happy Traum, all Oak Pubs.). Moreover, the music theory presented has been minimal as far as possible since it is adequately covered in other books (for instance *A Folksinger's Guide to Note Reading and Music Theory* by Jerry Silverman, Oak Pubs.).

The material in this book is graded in difficulty and can be used with or without an instructor. If it is used without a teacher, however, it is best to have access to some guitar-playing friends and a reasonable record collection. In many cases only listening can clarify certain subtle points that would take many pages to describe in a book.

Due to copyright changes, Figures 86-101 have been omitted from this book.

THE BARE BEGINNINGS

INTRODUCTION

Where to begin an instruction book is a difficult decision for an author. I will begin this book by answering some of the questions most commonly asked by beginning guitar students.

What kind of guitar should I use? Yes, preferably with all six strings intact. Most traditional musicians learned to play on guitars worse than anything you could possibly buy today no matter how little (or how much) you are willing to pay. Expensive guitars are usually easier to play. Nylon strongs are easier to play than steel but are rarely used in traditional music. Nylon strings are best for learning but must be exchanged for steel strings before any serious effort is made to learn traditional techniques. Conclusion: get the best guitar you can afford, but in reality just about anything will do.

How do I tune a guitar? Take your guitar to a friend and have him tune it for you!! There is no way one can learn to tune a guitar from a book alone unless he knows what it should sound like when it is "in tune." After some familiarity with the sound of the correctly tuned guitar has been gained, the student can refer to the Appendix on tuning for the most common methods of tuning the guitar. If you feel brave, you can try it now.

Should I play chords or notes? Accompaniments consist of more chords than notes, and solos usually consists of more notes than chords. Since we're mainly interested in instrumental solos, we will pay particular attention to notes, but we will also be learning all the necessary chords in the process. One of the basic principles of this book is not to learn any chord until we have a use for it. For this reason this entire volume uses only three basic chords!!

OK, what do I do first? Here we really begin. Look at the photo in Figure 1 and see how to hold the guitar. Also look at some of the other photos in this book and see how other guitarists hold their guitars. You will probably tend to hold the guitar so that you can see what your hands are doing. This is tolerable for a beginning, but must be corrected before any serious playing will be done. Work on the techniques we will be learning until they can be played with your eyes closed. This will seem difficult at first but most things will take no more than five or ten minutes to learn so that they can be played with closed eyes. Then you will be able to hold the guitar correctly with no restriction on playing.

In Figure 2 we have outlined some of the major parts of the guitar. When you hold the guitar, the face should be almost vertical.

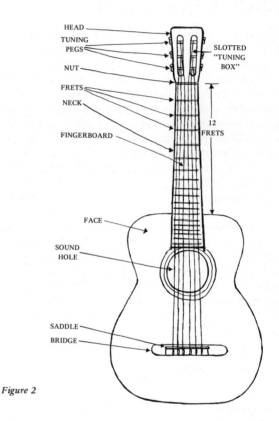

Figure 2

Also notice that the "top string," that is, the highest pitched string of the guitar, is nearest the floor and the "bottom string," the lowest pitch; when we speak of "up the neck," the direction indicated is from the tuning machines toward the body of the guitar, thus the direction of increasing pitch on the strings.

We will begin learning only two chords, called C and G7 (pronounced "Cee" and "Gee-Seven" or "Gee-Seventh") which are probably the two most useful chords in traditional folk guitar playing. Work on learning these two chords while learning the introductory material in the rest of Chapter 1. Then, by the end of Chapter 1 you will know these chords and will be ready to progress further. In the next chapter we will already be playing instrumental solos using only these two chords.

THE FIRST CHORD — C

In order to represent chords in a book we need some sort of shorthand notation because using a photo of a guitar doesn't always look right. In Figure 3 we show a progression from a sketch of a guitar on the far left, to what we will call a chord diagram on the far right. The chord diagram is simply a schematic view of a portion of the guitar as seen from the top. We will use the chord diagram to show where we are to put our fingers on the guitar. Notice that the first string, or the highest pitched string, is to the right in the diagram and the lowest pitched string is on the left. Thus we can see that the

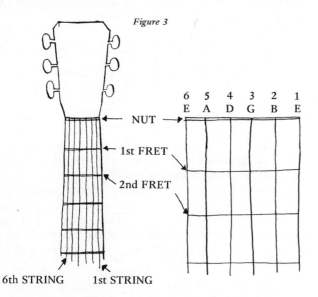

Figure 3

vertical lines represent the strings and the horizontal lines represent the frets of the guitar. (Frets are the metal inserts on the guitar neck perpendicular to the strings.)

STEP ONE: Place the index finger of your left hand in the position shown in the chord diagram in Figure 4 and the sketch in Figure 5. This is on the second string at the first fret. Place the tip of the left hand

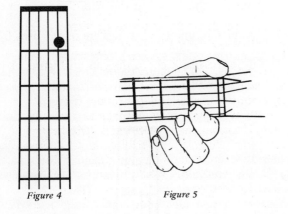

Figure 4   Figure 5

index finger (with a relatively short fingernail) just in back of the first fret of the second string. Now push

the string down with the finger tip so that the string is held tightly against the metal fret as shown in Figure 6.

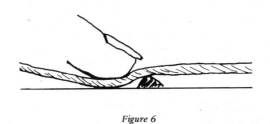

Figure 6

STEP TWO: Pluck the second string with the thumb of the right hand so that it is allowed to sound. It should sound true and clear. (This is a very subjective judgement and is best made by comparing the sound of your strings to other guitar players.) The sound should have the same quality (but not the same *pitch*) as when the same string is plucked with the index finger of the left hand removed from the string (an unfretted string is referred to as "open"). The *tone quality* of the "fretted" and "open" string should be almost the same.

STEP THREE: While fretting the second string at the first fret as described in Step Two, above, sound the first and third strings with the thumb. These strings would be open; in other words, the index finger of the left hand, while fretting the second string, should not touch either the first or third strings. They should sound exactly the same when the second string is fretted and when the second string is left open. If this is not the case you must adjust the position of the index finger on the second string until only the second string is being touched by it.

STEP FOUR: Use the second finger of the left hand to fret the fourth string at the second fret as shown in the chord diagram in Figure 7 and the sketch in Figure 8. You must go through the same procedure as above except now you must make sure that both

Figure 7   Figure 8

the second *and* fourth strings are properly fretted at the same time. The first and third strings must remain open—this is indicated in the chord diagram in Figure 7 by the two little zeros at the top of the open strings. Make sure that when you put down the second finger to fret the fourth string you are not disturbing the fretting of the second string.

STEP FIVE: While holding down the two fingers, as in the above steps, use the third finger to fret the fifth string at the third fret as shown in the chord diagram in Figure 9 and the sketch in Figure 10. You must repeat the same steps and cautions as in the above step.

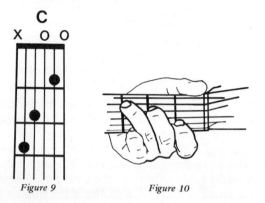

Figure 9   Figure 10

Notice the capital C above the chord diagram. This indicates that this is the complete C chord. Also notice the little "x" above the sixth string. This means that that string is not used in this chord and should not be sounded when playing this chord.

STEP SIX: The whole chord is now "sounded" in the following way: with the thumb of the right hand sound the fifth string, allowing the thumb to rest on the fourth string, etc. In this way one has enough time to hear and evaluate the sound of each string in the chord before hearing the next note.

Now, no matter how good or bad the chord sounds. . . .

Take a five minute break and relax.

After you've worked the cramp out of your hand, go through the above six steps again slowly. If one note sounds bad, stop and figure out what's wrong. Usually, a slight movement of a finger of the left hand will solve many problems:

Symptom: String sounds muffled but has the correct pitch.
Cause: Finger too far back from the fret and string not held tightly enough.
Cure: Move finger closer toward the fret.

Symptom: String buzzes but finger is in correct position.
Cause: Finger not fretting string tightly enough.
Cure: Push harder. Also try pushing harder with the thumb on the back of the guitar neck.

Symptom: An open string sounds dead or muffled.
Cause: The open string is being touched by a finger or some other part of the hand.
Cure: Remove the responsible finger.

Symptom: Everything's right but it still doesn't sound right.
Cause: Fingernails too long.
Cure: Cut.

Symptom: Too many strings are touched by one finger.
Cause: Fat fingers.
Cure: Use the tip of the finger for fretting. The "flat" of the finger (the part with the fingerprint) will be used when two or more strings will have to be fretted by one finger, so even fat fingers have their uses.

Questions:

You will find many sequences of questions interspersed throughout the text in the first few chapters of this volume. They are not intended to be "quizzes" or "tests" of what you have learned. They are meant to solidify in your own mind, using your own words and actions, what we have been discussing. You will find that you will learn faster and remember more by using and answering the questions as they arise in the text. If you cannot answer a certain question go back in the text and find the answer before going on to the next section. Answers to the questions are at the end of the individual chapters. Check all answers before going on. Also, occasionally some new material will be presented in the questions, so don't get too frightened.

1—What do the vertical lines represent in the chord diagram? _____

2—What are the horizontal lines in the chord diagram? _____

3—The string farthest to the left in the chord diagrams is the _____th string.

4—The string at the far right of the diagram is the _____st string.

5—What do the black dots in the chord diagram mean? _____

6—What do the "o's" in the chord diagram mean? _____

7—Completely unplayed strings are represented by an _____

8—Fill in the blank chord diagram in Figure 11 with a C chord.

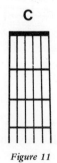

Figure 11

9—Which finger frets the second string? _____
10—Which finger frets the fourth string? _____
11—Which finger frets the third string? _____
12—Which finger is used on the first fret? _____
13—Which finger is used on the third fret? _____
14—How many strings are used in the C chord? _____
15—How many open strings are used in the C chord?

_____

16—Which are they? _____
17—How many strings are fretted in the C chord?

_____

18—Which ones? _____
19—Which finger is used to fret the second fret?

_____

20—Where is the third finger used? _____
21—Which string is not played in the C chord? _____

AIDS TO LEARNING CHORDS

1. Hold the C chord in your best possible form. Now "freeze" your fingers and remove your whole hand from the guitar, still retaining the fingers as if they were playing the C chord. Feel how your fingers are held. Feel the shape of your hand. Now slowly replace the hand on the guitar, press the fingers into position and strum the chord to make sure your fingers haven't moved. Repeat at least five times. This should be done for several days after encountering any new chord. It helps your hand "remember" the chord.

2. With your hand held about six inches above the guitar neck, form what you think is as close to the C chord as possible. Now, without rearranging your fingers relative to each other, slowly place them on the guitar fingerboard. If they are not in the correct positions, move your fingers one at a time, noting which way they are being moved until they are in the correct C chord position. Repeat until you can correctly form the C chord without the aid of the guitar. In this way you assure that the knowledge of the chord position is completely in you and not partially a part of the guitar.

Take a five minute break.

THE SECOND CHORD — G7

The G7 chord is the only other chord that we will be learning in this chapter. We will go through the same steps in learning the G7 chord that we did in learning the C chord but a little more quickly.

STEP ONE: Place the index finger of your left hand on the first string at the first fret as shown in Figures 12 and 13. Be sure that the index finger is not touching the second string.

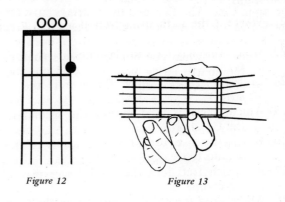

Figure 12 *Figure 13*

STEP TWO: Sound the first string (fretted), the second, third and fourth strings (open).

STEP THREE: Place the second finger of the left hand on the fifth string at the second fret as shown in Figures 14 and 15. Test the five strings to make sure all is well.

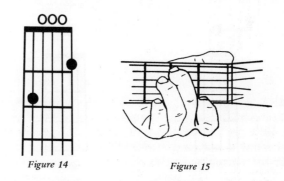

Figure 14 *Figure 15*

STEP FOUR: Now add the third finger fretting the sixth string at the third fret as shown in Figures 16 and 17. This is now the completed G7 chord. Sound

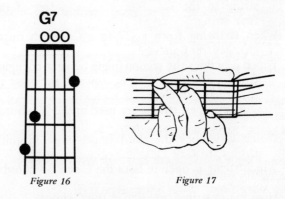

G7

Figure 16 *Figure 17*

all six strings and make corrections where necessary. Repeat the exercises for learning chords used for the C chord.

Questions:

22—Where is the sixth string fretted in the G7 chord? _____

23—Which finger is used to play the first string in the G7? _____

24—In the *C chord*, which finger frets the second string? _____

25—Which finger is used to fret the second fret in the G7 chord? _____

26—Which finger is used in the C chord to fret the second fret? _____

27—At which fret does the third finger play in the G7 chord? _____

28—Where does the third finger play in the C chord? _____

29—How many strings are used in the C chord? _____

30—Which string does the third finger play in the G7 chord? _____

31—How many strings are used in the G7 chord? _____

32—Fill in the diagrams in Figures 18 and 19.

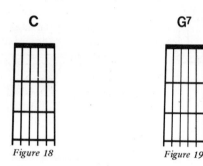

C   G7

Figure 18   *Figure 19*

33—When changing from a C chord to a G7 chord, the second finger moves from the fourth string to the _____ string.

34—When changing from a C chord to a G7, the index finger goes from the first fret of the second string to the _____ fret of the first string.

35—When changing from a G7 to a C, which finger changes fret number? _____

36—Which way does the second finger move in changing from a G7 to a C (i.e., toward the bass or toward the treble)? _____

37—How many open strings are used in the G7 chord? _____

38—Which way does the third finger move in going from C to G7? _____

39—Which string is open in both the C and G7 chords? _____

40—How many strings are used in the C chord? _____

41—Which way does the index finger move in going from G7 to C? _____

42—Which way does each of the following fingers move in going from the C to the G7 chords?
Index from *1st fret, 2nd string* to _____
Second from _____ to *2nd fret, 5th string*
Third from _____ to _____

43—Which finger changes fret number in going from G7 to C? _____

AIDS TO LEARNING CHORD CHANGES

1. Play the C chord. Tell each finger out loud where it should go in order to change to the G7 chord. Move the finger as directed. Repeat, but go from the G7 chord to the C chord. Repeat at least five times. Then try telling two fingers where to move and move them at the same time. Finally, move all three fingers at the same time from the C to the G7 and from the G7 to the C chords.

2. Play the C chord. Remove the left hand from the guitar without losing the position of the C chord. In the air, change the hand position from the C chord to the G7 chord. Now replace your hand on the guitar and check the hand position. Repeat, going from the C to the G7 and from the G7 back to the C chord. Repeat until the changes are correct.

Take a five minute break.

GUITAR NOTATIONS AND TABLATURE

The notations in this book will be given in standard music notation and tablature. The music will not be discussed since the tablature is easier to use for the beginning guitar student. If the student is already familiar with music, it can be used satisfactorily. If the student is interested in learning to read notes on the guitar he is referred to *A Folksinger's Guide to Note Reading and Music Theory* by Jerry Silverman, Oak. We will be dealing only with an explanation of tablature.

Tablature may be explained as follows. The six horizontal lines of the tablature, as shown in Figure 20, represent the six strings of the guitar. The highest pitched, the first string, corresponds to the top line

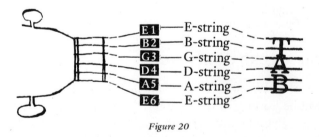

Figure 20

of the tablature. The second string is represented by the second line. Similarly for the other strings.

Now that we have a method of indicating which strings are to be played, all we need is a way of indicating the frets. We can number the frets in the following way: zero corresponds to an open string, one corresponds to a string fretted at the first fret, etc. Now we can write the fret number to be played *on* the string (or line) to be played in the tablature.

10

Now, by using the rules for tablature, let us decipher the tablature shown in Figure 21. First the large capital TAB means we are reading tablature (and not music) so we can proceed from there. The upper

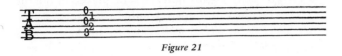

Figure 21

most line (corresponding to the first string) has a zero written on it, thus the first string is to be sounded open, i.e. not fretted. The second line has a number one on it indicating that the second string is to be fretted at the first fret. The zero on the third line shows the third string to be sounded open. The fourth string is stopped at the second fret and the fifth string at the third fret. The sixth string is not to be played since nothing is indicated on it. If you will hold down all the indicated notes at one time you will find that this corresponds to a C chord—which we already know.

Since all the numerals in the tablature are written in a vertical row, they are all to be sounded at the same time. Tablature, as normal writing, is read serially from left to right.

Questions:

44—What do the lines of the tablature represent?

_____

45—What does the top line of tablature mean? _____

_____

46—The bottom line? _____

47—From the tablature in Figure 22 fill in the table.

Figure 22

a—String _____ ; Fret _____
b—String _____ ; Fret _____
c—String _____ ; Fret _____
d—String _____ ; Fret _____
e—String _____ ; Fret _____
f—String _____ ; Fret _____

48—In the blank tablature given in Figure 23, fill in a G and C chord.

Figure 23

TIMING AND LENGTH

Only one thing more remains to be discussed about the reading of tablature for the guitar and this is timing. Both tablature and music are divided into rhythmic units by vertical lines called *bars* or *bar lines.* The divisions produced by the bar lines are called *measures.*

The two numbers at the beginning of the music and tablature are called the *time signature* which indicates the total time value of each measure. Thus, if all the time were added up it must equal the value indicated by the time signature for each measure.

The lower number of the time signature tells the time value of each beat or count. The quarter note will be used as the rhythmic unit for most of the music in this book. Unless otherwise specified you can take a quarter note to be equal to one beat.

The upper number of the time signature indicates the number of such counts or beats per measure. For instance, the time signature $\frac{2}{4}$ shows that there are 2 counts per measure and each count receives the time value of a quarter note. The time signature $\frac{4}{4}$ indicates that there are four quarter notes per measure. The time signature $\frac{3}{4}$ shows that there are three quarter notes per measure.

Questions:

49—The vertical lines in the tablature are called _____

_____

50—They divide the tablature into _____
51—Do all measures have the same time value? _____
52—What are the two large numbers at the beginning of the music and tablature called? _____

_____

53—What is its purpose? _____
54—What does the upper number signify? _____

_____

55—The lower number? _____
56—How is the total time value of each measure indicated? _____
57—A measure of $\frac{2}{4}$ time receives _____ beats.
58—Each beat in a measure of $\frac{2}{4}$ time is a _____ note.
59—The time signature for music which consists of 4 beats per measure and each beat receives the length of a quarter note would be _____ time.
60—What does the 3 of " $\frac{3}{4}$ " mean? _____
61—What does the 4 mean? _____
62—How many beats in each measure of $\frac{4}{4}$ time? _____
63—In $\frac{3}{4}$ time, how many beats per measure? _____

Take a five minute break and practice chords.

Since tablature cannot conveniently indicate a note value longer than a quarter note, we will use the quarter as a basis for longer notes. Just as notes are named after numerical fractions, they also add like fractions. The addition of two notes is indicated by a *tie*, a curved line joining the two notes whose time values are to be summed. This is illustrated in Figure 24 where two

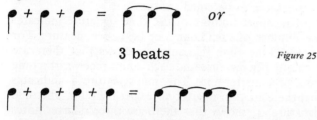

Quarter note   two beats

Figure 24

quarter notes are tied to form a note that has a time value equal to two beats; it is thus called a half note. Similarly, we can, by addition of quarter notes, get notes of three beat or four beat duration as shown in Figure 25.

3 beats

Figure 25

4 beats

Again, as in fractions, note values of less than one quarter are indicated by correspondingly smaller fractions. Thus, a note receiving only half the time value of a quarter note is called an eighth note. An eighth note is indicated by a *flag* attached to its stem as shown in Figure 26. A note of time value one half that of an

Eighth note   *Figure 26*   Sixteenth note

eighth note is called a sixteenth note and is indicated by two flags as shown in the second portion of Figure 26.

When eighth notes follow each other it is customary to join their flags into a *beam*. This does not combine the time values of the two eighth notes as does the tie; this is shown in Figure 27.

but   Tie   *or*

Beam   *Figure 27*

Questions:

64—How many quarter notes equal a half note? _____

65—How many quarter notes are needed to form a whole note? _____

66—How many eighth notes can be played in the time ascribed to a quarter note? _____

67—One can say that 1 quarter note equals _____ eighth notes.

68—How many quarter notes are played in a measure of $\frac{4}{4}$ time? _____

69—How many quarter notes are needed to form a half note? _____

70—How many half notes can be played in a measure of $\frac{4}{4}$ time? _____

71—How many whole notes are played in a measure of $\frac{4}{4}$ time? _____

72—How many half notes can be played in a measure of $\frac{2}{4}$ time? _____

73—How many eighth notes equal one quarter note? _____

74—How many quarter notes can be played in a measure of $\frac{3}{4}$ time? _____

75—What is the maximum number of eighth notes in a $\frac{3}{4}$ measure? _____

76—In a G7 chord the second finger plays the _____ string.

77—Which of the measures in Figure 28 are wrong? _____

Figure 28

Silences or *rests* in music notation and tablature are indicated in the same way as notes. The quarter rest (𝄽) is the basis and is a silence of the same time value as a quarter note. Other rests correspond to the associated note time values: eighth rest (𝄾), a sixteenth rest (𝄿), a half rest (▬).

Most of the music in this volume of *Playing Folk Guitar* will use only quarter notes, eighth notes and quarter rests. This simplifies matters considerably. And for the rest of this chapter we will be concerned only with quarter notes in $\frac{4}{4}$ time. This consists of an even count per measure of 1, 2, 3, 4, just like marching.

TOM DOOLEY — READING MELODIES

We will now learn to play the melody of a song on the guitar. The reason for this is that one must first know how a song should sound before he can play an instrumental solo. Many of the songs which we will use as instrumental solos in this book are accompanied by the melody of the song written out separately. Thus, if you do not know the melody of a song, you should learn it before attempting the instrumental solo.

We have now learned enough about tablature and timing to read a melody and to play it on the guitar. Look at the tablature of the song *Tom Dooley* given below. Notice that the whole melody consists of only quarter notes and, at the end, two quarter rests.

Tom Dooley - Melody

Hang down your head Tom Doo - ley Hang down your head and cry.____

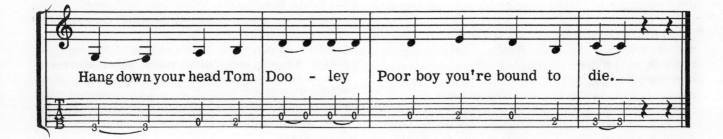

Hang down your head Tom Doo - ley Poor boy you're bound to die.____

STEP ONE: Temporarily ignoring the timing of the first measure, we will learn the position of the notes on the guitar. The first note of the song is on the sixth string at the third fret. (Remember that the bottom line of the tablature represents the sixth or lowest pitched string and the number three means that it is to be played at the third fret). The first note is shown in the chord diagram in Figure 29 and the sketch in Figure 30. This note should be fretted with the third

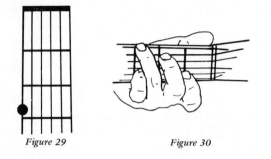

Figure 29   Figure 30

finger of the left hand. Sound this note—it is the first note of the melody line of *Tom Dooley*. The second note is the fifth string open. Sound this note. The final note of the first measure is the fifth string at the third fret. Simply move your third finger from the sixth string to the fifth string as shown in Figures 31 and 32.

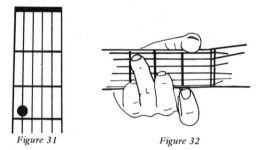

Figure 31   Figure 32

Sound the third note. Do this several times until the three notes can be played comfortably without hesitation or stumbling.

STEP TWO: Now let us look at the rhythm alone, without worrying about the melody. The time signature tells us that there are four beats per measure, each beat corresponding to a quarter note. Thus we simply count: 1, 2, 3, 4. The first two quarter notes are tied together to form a half note, this occupies beats one and two. The remaining two quarter notes are on beats 3 and 4, respectively. If we were to clap the rhythm of the first measure, you could clap on counts 1, 3, and 4, or 1(x), 2( ), 3(x), 4(x), where the x's represent claps. Tap your foot in a regular rhythm, count out loud 1, 2, 3, 4, and clap on beats 1, 3, and 4. This is

the rhythm of the first measure.

STEP THREE: Now let's put the melody and the rhythm together. On count *one*: hold the sixth string at the third fret with the thumb of the right hand. On count *two*: do nothing (the length of the half note is two beats). On count *three*: sound the fifth string open. On count *four*: sound the fifth string at the third fret. Repeat this until the measure can be played smoothly. This will usually take between five and twenty repetitions.

Now repeat this whole procedure with each measure individually up to the last measure. Then try larger sections of the song, such as two measures at a time, then three measures at a time. Finally you should try to play the whole melody of *Tom Dooley* which should, by now, sound something like the melody to *Tom Dooley*.

Recommended Listening:

Whenever recordings of the songs we are studying are available played by folk performers, I have included some records which might prove helpful in studying the melodies and, in some cases, the solos. Whenever possible, you should take the time to locate and listen to at least one of the recordings listed.

New Lost City Ramblers, Volume 2, Folkways FA 2397.
Doc Watson, Vanguard VSD-79152.
Paul Clayton — Bloody Ballads, Riverside RLP 12-615.

Questions:

78—Which finger should be used to fret the first note of the second measure? _____
79—Which finger should be used to fret the first note of the third measure? _____
80—The last note of the fifth measure? _____
81—The second note of the seventh measure? _____
82—The last note of the seventh measure? _____
83—How many strings of the guitar are used in this song? _____
84—List them: _____
85—How many different frets are used in this song? _____
86—List the frets used: _____
87—How many measures have rhythm the same as the first measure? _____
88—Which are they? _____
89—How many measures have rhythm the same as the second measure? _____
90—Which are they? _____
91—How many different rhythmic patterns are represented in this song? _____
92—List them:
    1—half, quarter, quarter
    2—_____
    3—_____
    4—_____

93—What does the upper number of the time signature signify? _____

94—How many measures are in this song? _____

95—How many quarter notes are equal to a half note? _____

96—In a C chord, which finger frets the fourth string? _____

97—In a G7 chord, how many strings are open? _____

TOM DOOLEY — ACCOMPANIMENT FOR A MELODY

Now that we have learned to plunk out the melody of a song on the guitar, we will learn to accompany this melody when it is sung. You can use the guitar melody as an aid in finding the right notes to sing in learning the melody. (Even if you have a very bad voice, as does the author, this method will lead to an acceptable, if not beautiful, result.) Play the melody on the guitar and sing the words simultaneously until you can sing the words without the aid of the guitar.

The basic accompaniment that we will be learning will consist of a bass note and of a chord. In Chapter 2 of this volume we will use exactly the same bass notes and the same chords to play instrumental solos in the style of the Carter Family. By learning this basic accompaniment here, we will be well equipped to undertake the problems of playing instrumental solos in the next chapter.

Let us spend a few minutes getting our right hand in the correct position for picking the guitar strings. We will start from a position that we all know—the right handed hitch-hiking position. In Figure 33 we see the hand in the correct starting position. Notice how

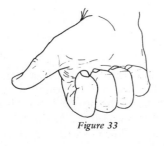

Figure 33

the thumb is extended away from the fingers. This is very important. Now simply lower the whole hand, without changing the position of the fingers or the thumb down toward the face of the guitar over the sound hole; this is shown in Figure 34. Notice that

the thumb is now extended right along the fifth string.

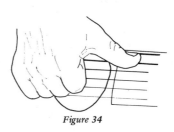

Figure 34

The next step is to uncurl the little finger and rest it on the face of the guitar just behind the sound hole as shown in Figure 35. This is not absolutely necessary

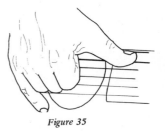

Figure 35

but it will steady your hand when picking. If you find it terribly uncomfortable try going ahead without anchoring the little finger, but you will probably want to use the anchor by the time we reach fingerpicking. Our hand, if it looks like the one shown in Figure 35, is now ready for accompanying a melody, Carter picking or fingerpicking. All these techniques use the same hand position, so learn it well.

The bass notes: We use the thumb of the right hand to sound bass notes in most of the guitar styles we will be studying. All notes to be played by the thumb are indicated in the tablature by the letter "T". For example, let us start by holding down the C chord and placing the thumb on the fifth string as shown in Figure 36. Now slowly start pushing the thumb toward the fourth string while it is still in contact with the fifth string. Let the side of the thumb slip off the fifth string toward the fourth string, letting the fifth string sound (at the third fret, of course). The thumb should come to rest on the fourth string as shown in Figure 37.

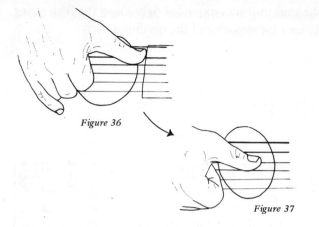

Figure 36

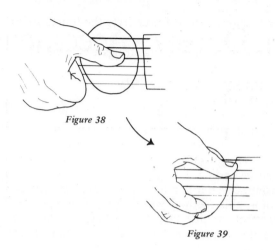

should stop moving just past the first string. Remember to keep the two fingers together during and after the brush as shown in the figures. Also notice that the top of the hand has not moved during the whole operation.

Figure 38

Figure 37

Figure 39

For the accompaniments used in this chapter, the thumb will always sound the fifth string in the C chord and the sixth string in the G7 chord.

The chord: The chord is sounded by the backs of the fingernails of the index and second fingers of the right hand brushing over the top three strings of the guitar. The hand position before the brush is shown in Figure 38 and after the brush has been completed in Figure 39. When the brush is completed, the fingers

The rhythm of the basic accompaniment in $\frac{4}{4}$ time is: thumb, brush, thumb, brush corresponding to the four beats of the measure as follows:

Beats: 1   2   3   4
Accompaniment: Thumb, brush, thumb, brush.

Thus on the first and third beats of each measure of accompaniment, the bass note is sounded and on the second and fourth beats the brushed chord is sounded. The brushed chord is represented in the tablature and music by the letter *B*. This is shown in an example of accompaniment below.

Below is the complete accompaniment to *Tom Dooley* with the words inserted. You should sing the melody we learned above and play the accompaniment given here at the same time. Make sure that the chord changes are smooth and the rhythm is even.

Tom Dooley - Accompaniment

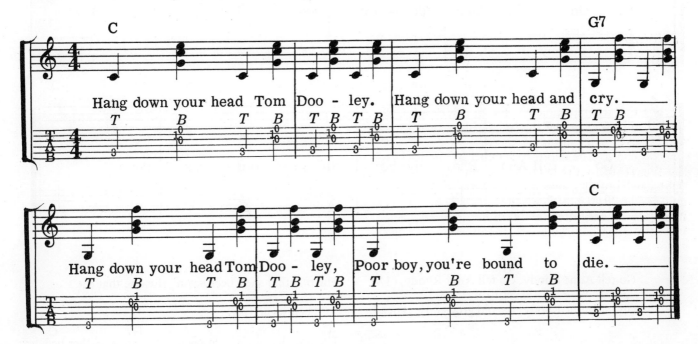

Questions:

98—The basic accompaniment consists of a _____ and a _____.

99—The first beat of the measure is occupied by the _____.

100—The second beat by the _____.

101—How many strings of the guitar does the C chord use? _____

102—How many fingers are used to play the brush? _____

103—On which beats of a measure of basic accompaniment does the thumb play a bass note? _____ and _____

104—The brush is played on which beats of the measure? _____

105—The bass note to be played in the C chord accompaniment is on the _____ string.

106—How much does the hand move during the basic accompaniment? _____

107—Which bass note is used in the G7 chord for basic accompaniment? _____

108—In the basic accompaniment to *Tom Dooley*, the word "head" corresponds to a thumb note or a brush note? _____

Take a five minute break.

GO TELL AUNT RHODY — PRACTICE

The following songs have been arranged to help you practice the techniques we have been learning. First find the notes of the melody on the guitar. Then look at the rhythm of each measure. Then put them together so that the melody can be played in rhythm on the guitar. Once you know the melody, sing the song using the basic accompaniment. Always make sure that the chord changes in the basic accompaniment are smooth and clean. Take all the songs slowly enough to make it sound neat. Once your playing is "clean," speed will come easily enough.

Since the basic accompaniment is a continuous thumb-brush pattern, it will not be written out each time for the following songs. Only the words will be written out with indications of where to change chords. Between this and a knowledge of the melody line of the song, you should have no difficulty with the accompaniment.

Recommended Listening:

Jean Richie — *Folk A-go-go*, Verve/Folkways 9011.

Go Tell Aunt Rhody - Melody

C   G7   C
Go tell Aunt Rhody, Go tell Aunt Rhody, (3X)
C   G7   C
Go tell Aunt Rhody, the old grey goose is dead.

C   G7
The one that she's been savin', the one that she's
             C
been savin' (3X)
C   G7   C
The one that she's been savin', to make a feather bed.

109—How many different strings of the guitar are used in this song? _____

110—How many different fingers are required to play it? _____

111—How many various rhythmic patterns are found? _____

112—How many rhythmic patterns in this song are the same as those used for *Tom Dooley*? _____

113—How many *new* rhythmic patterns are used in this song? _____

114—List them: _____ _____

Take a five minute break.

SKIP TO MY LOU — PRACTICE

The following songs are presented without comment and should provide enough practice to master the techniques in this chapter. Do not skip any of the songs; they are graded in difficulty and the hard ones come at the end of the chapter.

Recommended Listening:

Pete Seeger, *American Favorite Ballads*, Folkways FA 2030.
Washboard Band, Folkways FA 2201.

Questions:

115—How many strings are used to play the melody of this song? _____

116—Which string hasn't been used before? _____

117—How many *new* rhythmic patterns are used in this song?

118—List all the rhythmic patterns that occur in this song and their measures:
quarter, quarter, quarter, quarter in measures 1, 3, 5, 7, and 15 _____
_____
_____
_____

119—What is the left hand index finger used for in this song? _____

120—The second finger? _____

121—The third finger? _____

Skip To My Lou - Melody

Lost my part-ner what'll I do? lost my part- ner what'll I do?

Lost my part - ner what'll I do? Skip to my Lou, my dar - lin'.

Chorus

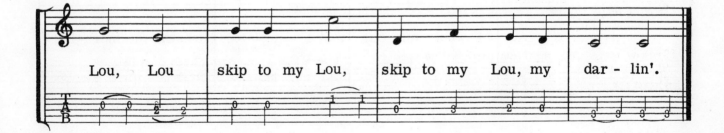

Lou, Lou, skip to my Lou: Lou, Lou skip to my Lou;

Lou, Lou skip to my Lou, skip to my Lou, my dar - lin'.

C	G7		C	G7
I'll get another one purtier'n you, I'll get another one,			Lost my partner, what'll I do? Lost my partner,	

purtier'n you,   what'll I do?

C   G7   C   G7
I'll get another one purtier'n you, Skip to my Lou,   Lost my partner, what'll I do? Skip to my Lou,

C   C
my darlin'.   my darlin'.

19

Recommended Listening:

> *Uncle Dave Macon,* RBF Records RF 51.
> *Horton Baker,* Folkways FA 2362.

Questions:

122—How many strings are used to play the melody of this song? _____

123—How many beats are in the first measure? _____

124—Does this violate the rules we have learned? _____

125—How many beats are in the last measure? _____

126—If we consider the first and last measures to be really one measure which has been split and part put at the beginning and part put at the end of the song, does the number of beats come out right? _____

127—What is the rhythmic pattern of the ninth measure? _____

Lolly Too Dum - Melody

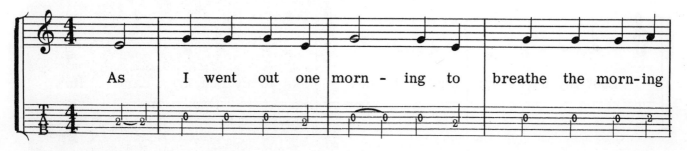

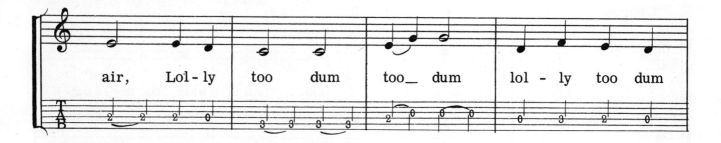

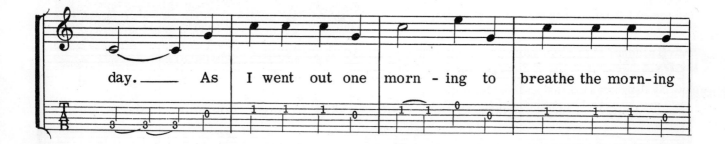

fair. Lol-ly too dum too— dum Lol-ly too dum day.

C
As I went out one morning to breathe the morning air,
        G7   C
Lolly too dum, too dum, lolly too dum day,
C
As I went out one morning to breathe the morning air,

I heard a dear old mother saying to her daughter fair,
          G7   C
Lolly too dum too dum lolly doo dum day.

Similarly:

You better go wash them dishes and hush your
    flattering tongue,
You know you want to marry and that you are
    too young.

O pity my condition, just as you would your own,
For fourteen long years I have lived all alone.

Supposing I were willing, where would you get
    your man?
Why, Lord mercy, mammy, I'd marry handsome Sam.

Supposing he would slight you like you done him
    before?
Why, Lord mercy, mammy, I'd marry forty more.

There's doctors and lawyers and men of high degree,
And some of them want to marry and some will
    marry me.

There's peddlers and tinkers and boys from the plow,
Lordy mercy, mammy, the fit comes on me now.

Now my daughter's married and well for to do,
Lordy mercy, boys, I'm on the market, too.

OLD JOE CLARK — PRACTICE

Recommended Listening:

New Lost City Ramblers — Volume 5, Folkways FA 2395.

Traditional Music At Newport—1964, Pt 2, Vanguard VSD-79183,

Washboard Band, Folkways FA 2201.

New Port Folk Festival—1960, Pt 1, Vanguard.

Woody Guthrie — Library of Congress, Elektra EKL-271/2.

George Pegram and Walter Parham — Pickin' and Blowin', Riverside RLP 12-650.

Wade Ward — *Banjo Songs from the Southern Mountains,* Prestige 25004.

Questions:

128—In the seventh measure, which string is used in the accompaniment for the first beat? _____

129—On the third beat of the same measure? _____

130—Which finger of the left hand is used to fret the third note of the melody? _____

Old Joe Clark - Melody

C
Old Joe Clark, the preacher's son, preached all over
  the plain,

                                          G7
The only text he ever knew was high-low, jack and
        C
    the game,
C   G7
Fare thee well Old Joe Clark, Fare thee well I say,
C   G7
He'll foller me ten thousand miles to hear my fiddle
      C
    play.

Old Joe Clark had a yellow cat, she would neither
      sing nor pray,
She stuck her head in a buttermilk jar and washed
      her sins away.

Old Joe Clark had a house fifteen stories high,
And every story of that house was filled with
      chicken pie.

CONCLUSION

In this chapter we have learned two things; to play a melody line on the guitar and to accompany a sung melody in a simple way. In the following chapters we will proceed to use the guitar in more and more complex ways. Wherever the melody lines are included with the songs they are intended to aid in the study of the instrumental solo of the song, they are not intended to be used as songs for themselves. If the student is interested in methods of accompanying folk songs he is referred to the appropriate books (for instance, Jerry Silverman's *Folksinger Guitar Guide*, Oak). We will now go on to learn to play solos on the guitar.

ANSWERS TO QUESTIONS

1—Strings.
2—Frets.
3—Sixth.
4—First.
5—Fingers.
6—Open strings.
7—No indication.
8—See text.
9—First finger.
10—Second finger.
11—None.
12—First finger.
13—Third finger.
14—Five.
15—Two.
16—First and third.
17—Three.
18—Second, fourth, fifth.
19—Second finger.
20—Third fret, fifth string.
21—Sixth string.
22—Third fret.
23—First finger.
24—First finger.
25—Second finger.
26—Second finger.
27—Third fret.
28—Fifth string, third fret.
29—Five
30—Sixth string.
31—All six.
32—See text.
33—Fifth string.
34—First fret.
35—None.
36—Toward the treble.
37—Three open strings.
38—Toward the bass.
39—Third string.
40—Five strings.
41—Toward the bass.
42—Index from second string, first fret to first string, first fret; second finger from 4th string, 2nd fret to 5th string, second fret; third finger from 5th string, 3rd fret to 6th string, 3rd fret.
43—None.
44—Strings.
45—First string
46—The sixth string.
47—a—5th string, 3rd fret.
　　b—1st string, open.
　　c—1st string, 1st fret.
　　d—6th string, 3rd fret.
　　e—4th string, 2nd fret.
　　f—5th string, 2nd fret.
48—See text.
49—Bar lines.
50—Measures.

51—Yes.
52—The time signature.
53—To indicate the pulse of the music.
54—Beats per measure.
55—Time value of the beat.
56—By the time signature.
57—Two.
58—Quarter note.
59—$\frac{4}{4}$ time.
60—3 beats per measure.
61—Each beat is a ¼ note.
62—Four.
63—Three.
64—Two.
65—Four.
66—Two.
67—Two.
68—Four.
69—Two.
70—Two.
71—One.
72—One.
73—Two.
74—Three.
75—Six.
76—Fifth string.
77—B and C are wrong.
78—Second finger.
79—Third finger.
80—Second finger.
81—Second finger.
82—Second finger.
83—Three strings.
84—4th, 5th, and 6th.
85—Two frets.
86—Second and third frets.
87—Two others.
88—3rd and 5th measure.
89—Two other measures.
90—4th and 6th measures.
91—Four.
92—a—½,¼,¼
　　b—½,½
　　c—¼,¼,¼,¼
　　d—½,¼ rest,¼ rest.
93—The number of beats per measure.
94—Eight.
95—Two quarter notes.
96—Second finger.
97—Three open strings.
98—Bass note and a brush note.
99—Bass note.
100—Brush note.
101—Five strings.
102—Two fingers.
103—Beats one and three.
104—Second and fourth beats.
105—Fifth string.
106—As little as possible.
107—6th string, 3rd fret.

108—Thumb.
109—Three strings.
110—Two fingers.
111—Five rhythmic patterns.
112—Three.
113—Two only.
114—Whole note and ¼,¼,½.
115—Four strings.
116—Second string.
117—None.
118—a—¼,¼,¼,¼ in 1, 3, 5, 7, 15.
　　　b—¼,¼,½ in 2, 4, 6, 10, 12, 14.
　　　c—½,½ in 8, 9, 11, 13, 16.

119—To fret the first fret.
120—Fret the second fret.
121—To fret the third fret.
122—Four strings.
123—Two.
124—See later questions.
125—Two.
126—Yes.
127—¾,¼.
128—Fifth string.
129—Sixth string.
130—Third finger.

CARTER STYLE SOLOS

INTRODUCTION

In this second chapter of this book, we will begin the study of guitar styles common to the Southern Mountains and used by the Carter Family. We will learn to play instrumental solos in this style by utilizing, with minor variations and additions, the material we learned in the last chapter: that is 1) how to play a melody and 2) how to play a thumb-brush accompaniment.

An instrumental solo is a mixture of melody and accompaniment. While the melody is being played, a form of accompaniment is played simultaneously. The basic differences between a solo and an accompaniment are: 1) an accompaniment is rhythmically regular but the solo must conform to the rhythm of the melody, 2) the single notes played in the accompaniment are simply the most convenient bass notes, but the notes played in the solo are the melody line itself, and 3) we have used chords for accompaniment, but

we have not used chords when we played the simple melody lines; in the solo we must hold the basic chord position on the guitar while playing the melody.

TOM DOOLEY — FIRST SOLO

Let us now consider our first solo in an elementary Carter style and see how the three observations above apply to this song. We are using *Tom Dooley* because we already know how to play the melody for this song and we also know how to accompany it. If you are not sure of both of these points, go back and review Chapter 1.

Before we play this song, let's look over the tablature and music in some detail. (You should always do this with an unfamiliar piece of music.)

Tom Dooley - First Solo

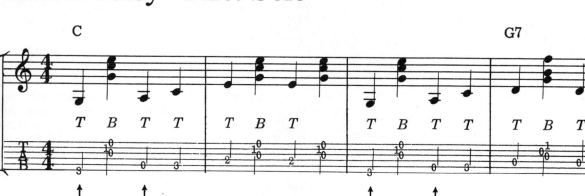

Let us first look at the rhythmic patterns required of the right hand. The basic accompaniment which we learned in Chapter 1 consisted of a regular thumb-brush-thumb-brush pattern. In our solo version of *Tom Dooley* you will notice that no such regular pattern exists. The first measure of the solo, for instance, is "thumb-brush-thumb-thumb." This is represented in the tablature and music by "T B T T." We cannot use the regular thumb-brush pattern because we are now playing an instrumental solo and not an accompaniment.

Questions:

1—What is the rhythmic difference between a solo and an accompaniment? _____
_____

2—How many different rhythmic patterns are used in the solo version of *Tom Dooley*? _____
_____

3—List them and the measures in which they occur.
   a—thumb-brush-thumb-thumb in measures 1, 3, and 5. _____
   b— _____
   _____
   c— _____
   _____

The second major difference between the solo and the accompaniment is that the solo contains all of the notes of the melody line of the song. Ignoring the chords and the brush in the solo version of *Tom Dooley* for the moment, look at the notes that are to be played by the thumb. You will notice that they are identical with the melody we learned for *Tom Dooley* in the previous chapter. Thus the solo does contain the melody of the song.

The third major difference between the solo and the accompaniment is the use of chords. For reasons that will be soon apparent, we must play the melody line while holding down the chords indicated in the music.

Let us now see what problems this last requirement entails. The music to *Tom Dooley* tells us to start by holding down a C chord. Notice that there are three bass strings that can be used for playing melody (the fifth string at the third fret, the fourth string at the second fret and the third string open). But the tablature tells us that the first note of *Tom Dooley* is to be played on the third fret of the sixth string! This is not one of the notes in the normal chord position for C. Thus it is called "out of the normal chord position."

In playing the melody notes in the guitar solos we will be studying, we will encounter three types of notes:

1—Notes that are *in the chord* position. These melody notes correspond to the notes that are found in the chord as it is normally held on the guitar. For the C chord these would be the fifth string at the third fret, the fourth string at the second fret and the third string open.

2—Notes that are *out of the chord* such as the first note of *Tom Dooley*. To get these notes we must move a finger out of the basic chord position. In this particular case, we move the third finger from the fifth string to the sixth string at the third fret. This position is illustrated in Figures 40 and 41.

3—Notes corresponding to open strings. This is illustrated by the note played on the third beat of the first measure of *Tom Dooley*, i.e., the fifth string open. To get these notes one simply lifts the finger which is fretting that particular string. In this case, it would be the third finger as shown in Figures 42 and 43.

Notice that the figures referred to above are shown in what is labeled a CHORD ANALYSIS BOX. In these boxes small portions of the songs under discussion are reproduced and the individual left hand positions are called out in detail in chord diagrams and in sketches. Thus one is given a detailed, "blow-by-blow" illustration of how to play that particular passage. CHORD ANALYSIS BOXES will be used extensively in Volume 2 of this series.

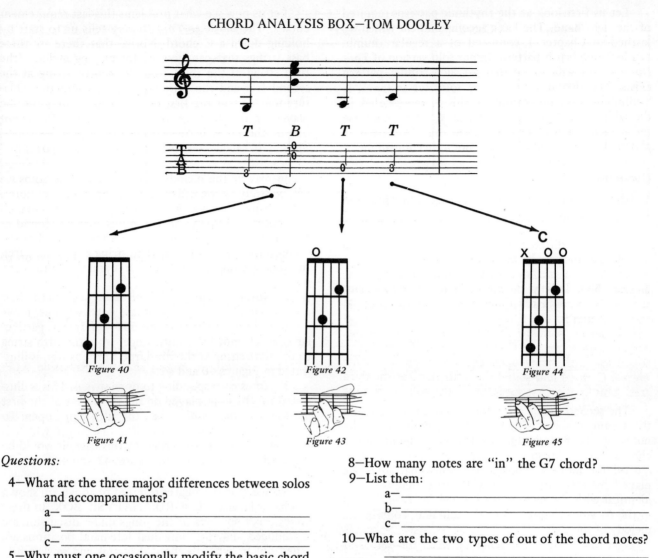

Figure 40

Figure 42

Figure 44

Figure 41

Figure 43

Figure 45

Questions:

4—What are the three major differences between solos and accompaniments?

a—_____

b—_____

c—_____

5—Why must one occasionally modify the basic chord position when playing the melody as an instrumental solo? _____

6—How many notes are "in the chord" in the C chord?

7—List them:

a—_____

b—_____

c—_____

8—How many notes are "in" the G7 chord? _____

9—List them:

a—_____

b—_____

c—_____

10—What are the two types of out of the chord notes?

_____

_____

11—In *Tom Dooley*, there are a total of six notes out of the basic chords. Arrows have been put under them. Find all six.

12—Recalling that we must change chords in the middle of *Tom Dooley*, fill in the following chart for the out of the chord notes:

28

	Measure	Chord	Lift Finger?	Move Finger?	Finger Used
a.—	1	C	No	Yes	third
b.—					
c.—					
d.—					
e.—					
f.—					

We are now ready to play through *Tom Dooley*. Remember the methods that we learned in the first chapter. First look at the rhythm; in the first measure it is ¼, ¼, ¼, ¼. Hold down the C chord. Move the third finger from the fifth string to the sixth string at the third fret. With the thumb sound the sixth string. Follow with a brushed C chord with the fingers. Then sound the fifth string open and finally return to the normal C chord and sound the fifth string at the third fret. This is the first measure of the solo version of *Tom Dooley*.

Repeat this until it is smooth and then go on to the next measure.

Recommended Listening:

New Lost City Ramblers — Volume 2, Folkways FA 2397.

Doc Watson, Vanguard VSD-79152.

Paul Clayton — *Bloody Ballads,* Riverside RLP-12-615.

Take a five minute break.

GO TELL AUNT RHODY — SECOND SOLO

In this song we will learn how to use the fourth (or little) finger of the left hand for fretting notes. We use the little finger to get notes on the third fret when we shouldn't move the third finger out of the basic chord position. The last note of the third measure of *Go Tell Aunt Rhody* is such a note; it is also illustrated in Figures 48 and 49 of the CHORD ANALYSIS BOX. (Notice that the measures which are analyzed are indi-

cated in the music and tablature in the solo by encirclement with a dotted line.) The use of the little finger must be learned before progressing to fingerpicking styles where the little finger is a major source of notes to be fretted out of the chords.

The rest of *Go Tell Aunt Rhody* should not be too difficult after careful study of the CHORD ANALYSIS BOX.

CHORD ANALYSIS BOX—GO TELL AUNT RHODY

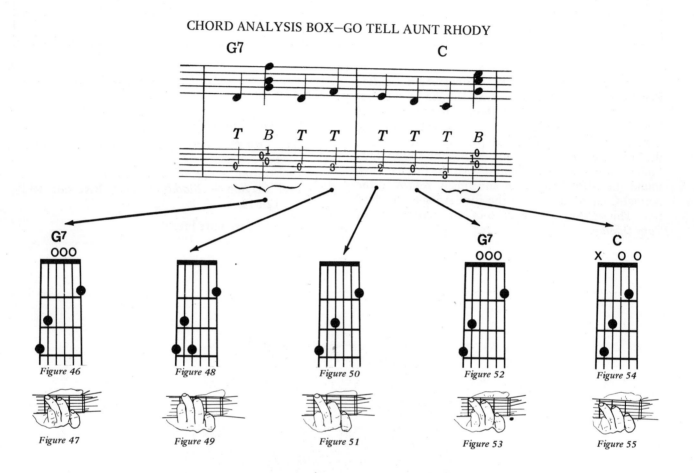

Figure 46

Figure 47

Figure 48

Figure 49

Figure 50

Figure 51

Figure 52

Figure 53

Figure 54

Figure 55

13—When is the little finger used to fret strings? _____
_____

14—Which finger is used to fret the fourth note of the fifth measure? _____

15—Which finger is used for the fourth note of the seventh measure? _____

16—Which finger is used for the second note of the seventh measure? _____

17—Are any new rhythmic patterns found in this song which were not found in *Tom Dooley*? _____
_____

18—List them:
a—_____
b—_____
c—_____

19—How many out of the chord notes are in this song?
_____

20—List them:
a—1st measure, 4th beat, 4th string, open
b—_____
c—_____
d—5th measure, _____
e—   2nd beat, _____
f—   4th string, _____

21—Which finger should be used to play the first note of the fourth measure? _____

22—Which finger for the second note of the seventh measure? _____

23—Which for the fourth note of the seventh measure?
_____

Recommended Listening:

Jean Richie — *Folk A-go-go*, Verve/Folkways 9011.

Go Tell Aunt Rhody - Solo

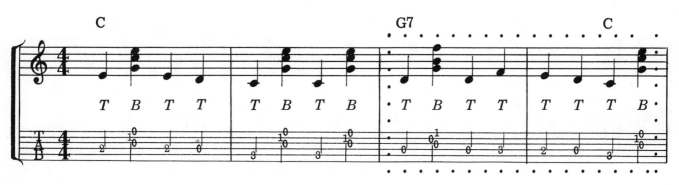

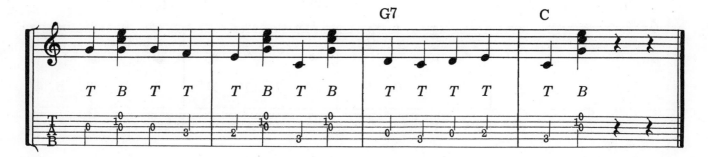

This song is not really as difficult as the previous song, but it is usually played faster. At this stage this will probably make it more difficult. Notice that the difficult part in the seventh measure is almost the same as the portion of *Go Tell Aunt Rhody* that was studied in that CHORD ANALYSIS BOX. You should always be on the look-out for similarities between songs so that you can efficiently utilize what you have already learned. For example, if you look at this solo measure by measure, you will find that you have already played most of the measures somewhere in one of the two previous solos.

Questions:

24—How many notes are out of the basic chords in this song? _____

25—Which finger should be used to fret the note on the third beat of the fourth measure? _____

26—On the second beat of the seventh measure? _____

27—On the third note of the seventh measure? _____

Recommended Listening:

Washboard Band, Folkways FA 2201.

Pete Seeger, *American Favorite Ballads,* Folkways FA 2030.

Skip To My Lou - Solo

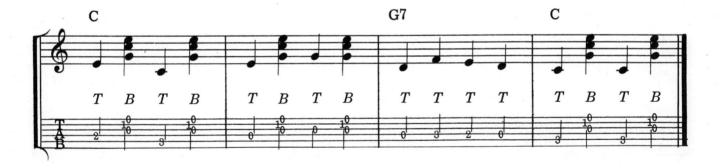

TOM DOOLEY — THE DOUBLE BRUSH

The double brush is one of the most basic rhythmic patterns in country guitar styles. To fully understand it and to learn it easily, we must begin with a short review.

Questions:

28—In a measure of $\frac{4}{4}$ time, what is the maximum number of quarter notes? _____

29—How many eighth notes "equal" a quarter note? __

30—How many eighth notes can be played in a $\frac{4}{4}$ measure? _____

31—What is the symbol for an eighth note? _____

32—How are two consecutive eighth notes indicated?

_____

In the first chapter we learned to count beats with the basic accompaniment in the following way:

Accompaniment: thumb, brush, thumb, brush
Count: 1, 2, 3, 4.

To include *eighth notes* in such a scheme, we divide the quarter note beat into two equal parts. The first of the pair of eighth notes is still represented by the number, but the second eighth note is represented by "&" (pronounced "and"). For example, let us look at a measure where the first quarter note has been divided into two eighth notes as illustrated in Figure 56. Notice that the beat is still even; if we were marching before to the count of 1, 2, 3, 4 we would still be marching to the same count, 1, 2, 3, 4. If the counts 1, 2, 3, 4 are one second apart, the 1 and the & would be ½ second apart and the & and the count 2 would also be a ½ second apart. Remember that two consecutive eighth notes can have their flags joined into a beam.

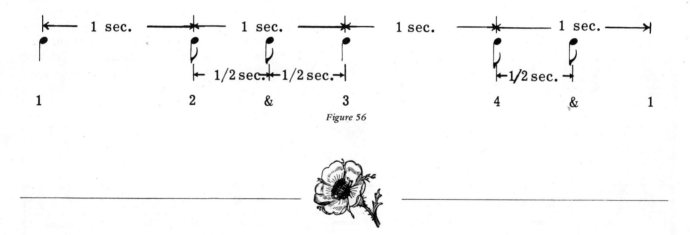

Figure 56

Questions:

33—Label the counts on ♪ ♪ ♩ ♩ ♩ , 1,&,2,3,4

34—♩ ♪ ♩ ♩

35—♩ ♩ ♪ ♪

36—♪ ♩ ♩ ♪ ♪

37—♩ ♫ ♩ ♩

38—♫ ♩ ♩ ♩

39—♩ ♫ ♩

40—♩ ♫ ♩ ♫

Now let us look at the pattern in that last question a little more closely since it is the one that we will be using in the double brush pattern. It is shown in Figure 57. Go over it carefully and be sure that you understand the rhythm represented.

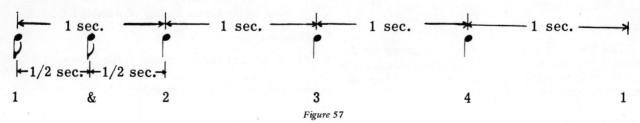

Figure 57

The above rhythmic pattern divides the second and fourth beats into two parts. The second and fourth beats correspond to the brushes in the basic accompaniment. Let us now see how they can be divided into two parts. The first brush note is the same as the one we have been using. It is a brush down with the backs of the fingernails of the first two fingers (see Figures 38 and 39).

The second brush note is new. It is a brush upward with the index finger alone. The sequence of motions required to play the second brushed note is illustrated by the following figures. After the first brush note has been completed, see Figure 58, and the tips of the first two fingers of the right hand extend slightly past the first string, then the index finger alone brushes up over the first few strings, as shown in Figure 59, and returns to its normal position as before the initial brush downward, Figure 60. During the upward brush, the index

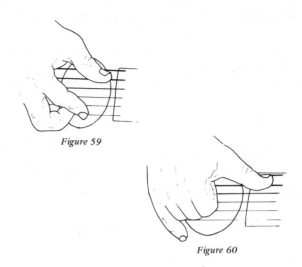

Figure 59

Figure 60

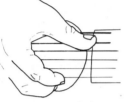

Figure 58

finger must relax until the knuckle in the finger bends backwards under the pressure of the string as shown above in the middle picture. *This is very important.* Only in this way will the second brush note be *softer* than the first brush. The downward brush is on the beat and the upward brush is off the beat and thus the former is rhythmically more important and should be slightly emphasized.

The whole double brush figure should become a smooth "down-up" motion of the fingers. The basic accompaniment in the C and G7 chords using the double brush is shown in the tablature.

Notice that the arrows indicate the direction of the brush. These will be omitted later where it is obvious which is the downward brush and which is the upward brush. *Remember: down with two fingers and up with one finger.*

Recommended Listening:

This list of records is intended as listening for developing the double brush. Any of the recordings will give ample illustration of the correct sound and emphasis of the single and the double brush.

The Famous Carter Family, Harmony 7280 ($1.98).
Collection of Favorites, Carter Family, Decca DL-4404.
Favorite Family Songs, Carter Family, Liberty 3230.
Great Original Recordings, Carter Family, Harmony HL-7300 ($1.98).
Original and Great, Carter Family, Camden CAL-586 ($1.98).
'Mid the Green Fields of Virginia, Carter Family, RCA Victor LPM-2772.
Keep On The Sunny Side, Columbia CL-2152.
Best of the Carter Family, Columbia CL-2319.

Questions:

41—How many fingers are used in the downward brush?

_____

42—How many in the upward brush? _____

43—Which fingers are used in the upward brush? _____

_____

44—In the basic accompaniment above, describe the technique used for each beat:
1—thumb, 2—_____, &—_____,
3—_____, 4—_____, &—brush-up

45—Which should be louder, the brush up or the brush down? _____

46—Why? _____

47—How is this difference in volume achieved? _____

_____

48—How does one test if the index finger is sufficiently relaxed? _____

49—Should the insertion of a double brush change the melody line of a solo? _____

Below we have our second version of *Tom Dooley* which has been arranged to include both single and double brushes. You should compare it, measure for measure, with the first version of *Tom Dooley* that we learned. Remember that smoothness in playing is much more important than speed.

On careful examination of the music, you should notice two changes (aside from the insertion of the double brushes) in this version of *Tom Dooley*. In the third beat of the next to last measure, a note that doesn't correspond to the melody has been added. This figure (the next to the last measure) is a very common pattern in Carter picking. In the last measure, the last note is a single downward brush held for the last three beats of the measure (indicated by the ties) and *not* three brushes.

Tom Dooley - Solo

GO TELL AUNT RHODY—MORE DOUBLE BRUSH

Our second version of *Go Tell Aunt Rhody* needs little introduction if the above version of *Tom Dooley* has been thoroughly studied. Its purpose is to provide more practice using double brushes. Again compare it to the previous version without the double brushes; compare not only the music but also the way the song sounds.

Go Tell Aunt Rhody - Solo

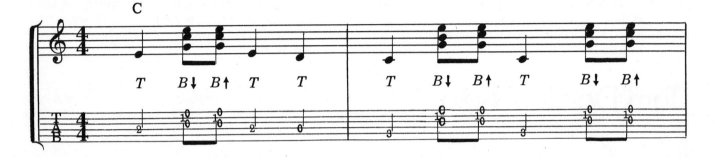

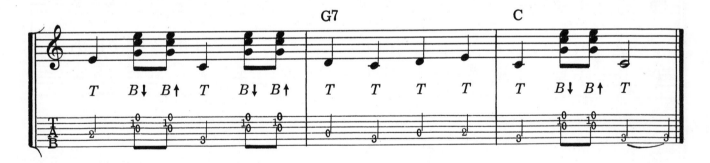

OLD JOE CLARK — NEW RHYTHMIC PATTERNS

You may have noticed that in all the songs we have learned, all the brushes or double brushes have occurred either on the second or the fourth beats of the measure. In this song we will introduce a new brush pattern which is seen in the fourth measure: thumb-brush-brush-thumb. Notice that this pattern contains two downward brushes. Do not confuse the two consecutive downward brushes with the double brush (down-up) figure which we just learned. The count of the new pattern in *Old Joe Clark* is 1, 2, 3, 4. This pattern, even though it is all quarter notes, provides an interesting rhythmic drive to *Old Joe Clark*.

36

Questions:

50—How many different rhythmic patterns are in this song? _____

51—Which finger should be used to fret the second note of the first measure? _____

52—The third note of the first measure? _____

53—The second note of the second measure? _____

Recommended Listening:

New Lost City Ramblers — Volume 5, Folkways FA 2395.

Traditional Music at Newport—1964, Pt 2, Vanguard VSD-79183.

Washboard Band, Folkways FA 2201.

Woody Guthrie — Library of Congress, Elektra EKL-271/3.

George Pegram and Walter Parham — *Pickin' and Blowin'*, Riverside RLP 12-650.

Wade Ward — *Banjo Songs from the Southern Mountains*, Prestige 25004.

Old Joe Clark - Solo

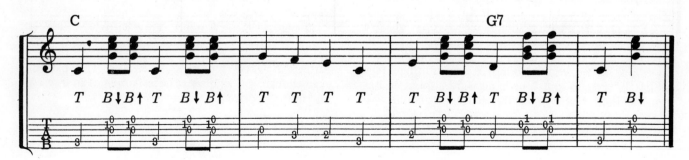

In this song we become even more free with our use of single and double brushes. Make sure to distinguish between two consecutive single brushes and a double brush.

Questions:

54—How many strings of the guitar are used to play this melody? _____

55—What is different about the eleventh measure? _____

56—Compare the rhythm of the second measure with the rhythm of the fifth measure.

57—Compare the rhythm of the fifth and ninth measures.

58—Compare the rhythm of the second and ninth measures.

59—Compare the rhythm of the ninth and the nineteenth measures.

60—Which finger should be used to fret the second note of the eighth measure? _____

Lolly Too Dum - Solo

This is our first song in ¾ or waltz time. You should have no difficulty in playing this tune if you keep in mind that the basic count for each measure is 1, 2, 3. If you are reading the music, recall that a note followed by a dot increases the note value by one half, thus the dotted half notes used in the melody of *Down In The Valley* are of three beat duration.

Down in the Valley - Melody

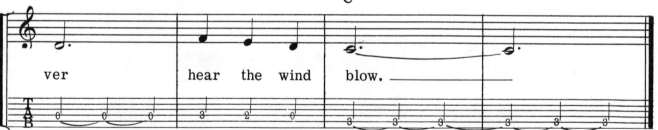

C   G7
Down in the valley, valley so low,

Hang your head over, hear the wind blow.
                                          C

Hear the wind blow, love, hear the wind blow,
Hang your head over, hear the wind blow.

If you don't love me, love whom you please,
Throw your arms 'round me, give my heart ease.

Give my heart ease love, give my heart ease,
Throw your arms 'round me, give my heart ease.

Write me a letter, send it by mail,
Send it in care of the Birmingham Jail.

Birmingham Jail, love, Birmingham Jail,
Send it in care of the Birmingham Jail.

Build me a castle, forty feet high,
So I can see her as she rides by.

Roses love sunshine, violets love dew,
Angels in heaven know I love you.

64—What does the bottom number of the time signature mean? _____

65—What does the top number mean? _____

66—How many quarter notes in a measure of $\frac{4}{4}$ time? _____

67—How many in a measure of $\frac{3}{4}$ time? _____

68—How many different rhythmic patterns are used in this song? _____

Recommended Listening:

Pete Seeger — *American Favorite Ballads*, Folkways FA 2030.

Cisco Houston — *Passing Through*, Verve/Folkways 9002.

Weavers — *Best of the Weavers*, Decca DXS B7-173.

Down in the Valley - Solo

This song will provide more practice in playing solos in waltz time using slightly more complex patterns. Be sure to play through the melody line several times so that you know what the solo should sound like.

Questions:

69—How many rhythmic patterns are used in this song?

_____

70—How many are different from those used in the previous song? _____

71—List them:

a— _____

b— _____

Recommended Listening:

Pete Seeger — *American Favorite Ballads*, Folkways FA 2030.

Peggy Seeger — *Folksongs of Courting and Complaint*, Folkways 49

Wagoner's Lad - Melody

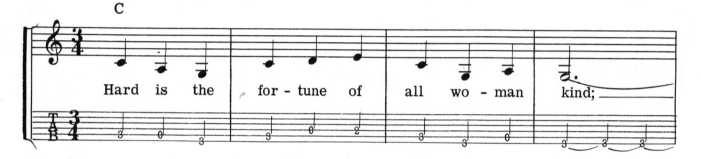

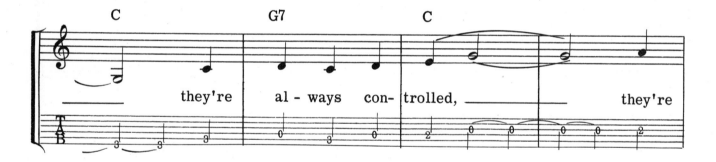

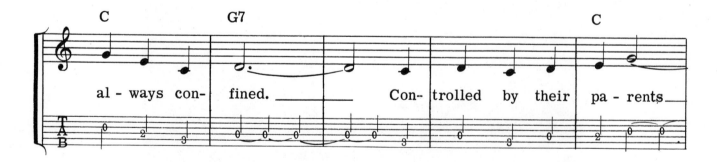

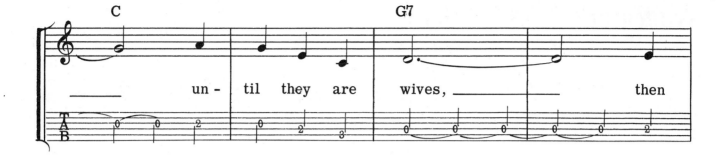

un - til they are wives, _____ _____ then

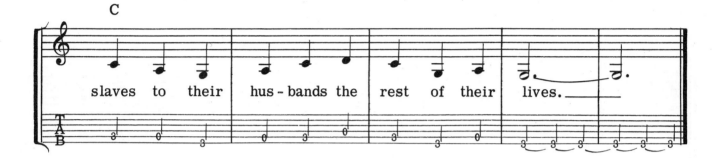

slaves to their hus - bands the rest of their lives. _____

C
Hard is the fortune of all woman kind,
   G7   C   G7
They're always controlled, they're always confined.
                    C   G7
Controlled by their parents until they are wives,
      C
Then slaves to their husbands the rest of their lives.

Oh, I am a poor girl, my fortune is sad,
I've always been courted by the wagoner's lad,
He courted me daily, by night and by day,
And now he is loaded and going away.

Your parents don't like me because I am poor,
They say I'm not worthy of entering your door.
I work for my living, my money's my own,
And if they don't like me they can leave me alone.

Your horses are hungry, go feed them some hay.
Come sit down beside me as long as you stay.
My horses ain't hungry, they won't eat your hay,
So fare thee well darlin', I'm goin' away.

Your wagon needs greasing, your whip is to mend,
Come sit down here by me as long as you can.
My wagon is greasy, my whip's in my hand,
So fare thee well darlin', no longer to stand.

Wagoner's Lad - Solo

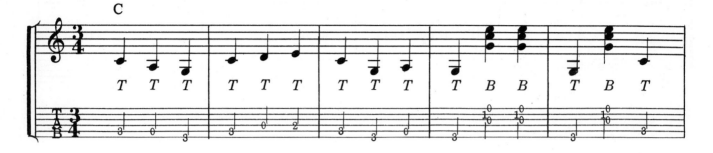

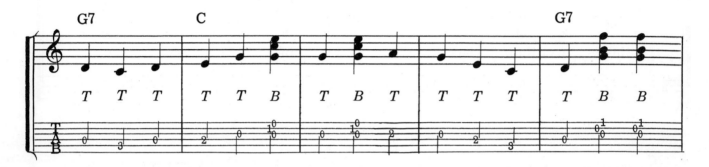

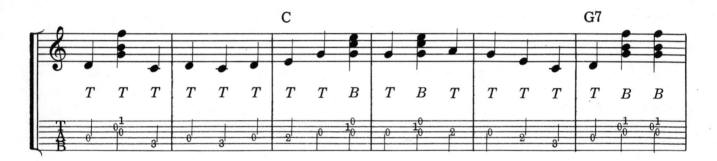

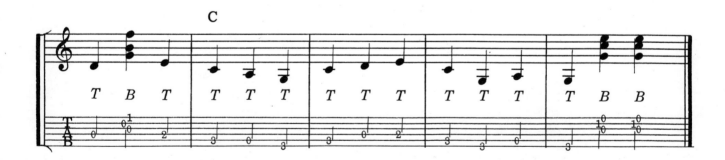

ANSWERS TO QUESTIONS

[For all unanswered questions, it's up to you.]

2—Three.
3—a—T,B,T,T, in 1,3,5.
   b—T,B,T,B, in 2,4,6.
   c—T,T,T,T, in 7.
6—Three bass notes.
7—a—5th string, 3rd fret.
   b—4th string, 2nd fret.
   c—3rd string, open.
8—Four bass notes.
9—a—6th string, 3rd fret.
   b—5th string, 2nd fret.
   c—4th string, open.
   d—3rd string, open.
12—a—1, C, No, Yes, third.
    b—1, C, Yes, No, third.
    c—3, C, No, Yes, third.
    d—3, C, Yes, No, third.
    e—5, G7, Yes, No, second.
    f—7, G7, No, Yes, second.
14—Little finger.
15—Second finger.
16—Little finger.
17—Yes.
18—T,B,T,T.
19—Six.
20—a—1st measure, 4th beat, 4th string, open.
    b—3rd measure, 4th beat, 4th string, 3rd fret.
    c—4th measure, 1st beat, 4th string, 2nd fret.
    d—5th measure, 4th beat, 4th string, 3rd fret.
    e—7th measure, 2nd beat, 5th string, 3rd fret.
    f—7th measure, 4th beat, 4th string, 2nd fret.
21—Second finger.
22—Little finger.
23—Second finger.
24—Three notes out of the chords.
25—Little finger.
26—Little finger.
27—Second finger.
28—Four quarter notes per measure.
29—Two eighth notes per quarter note.
30—Eight.
31—♪
32—♫
33—1, &, 2, 3, 4.
34—1, 2, &, 3, 4.
35—1, 2, 3, 4, &.
36—1, &, 2, 3, 4, &.
37—1, 2, &, 3, &, 4.

38—1, &, 2, 3, &, 4.
39—1, 2, 3, &, 4.
40—1, 2, &, 3, 4, &.
41—Two fingers.
42—Only the index finger.
43—Index.
44—T, B , B , T, B , B .
45—Downward brush.
49—No.
50—Four.
51—Second finger.
52—Little finger.
53—Little finger.
54—Five strings.
55—It uses the first string.
60—Little finger.
61—T, T, T, B , B , B , B , B , B , T, B , B .
62—1, 2, 3, 4, &; 1, &, 2, &, 3, 4, &.
63—It covers two measures.
68—Two rhythmic patterns.
69—Four rhythmic patterns.
70—Two new patterns.
71—a—Thumb, brush, thumb.
    b—Thumb, thumb, brush.

THE F CHORD

INTRODUCTION

When most folk guitarists refer to a musical "key," in most cases they are simply indicating the chords which they are using to accompany a song or the pitch of the song. Most commonly a key contains three chords within its structure. (A more accurate definition is given by any book on music theory like Jerry Silverman's *A Folksinger's Guide to Note Reading and Music Theory,* Oak, but we need no more precise definition to proceed at this point.) The chords in the key of C are C, F and G7. Thus we have been playing in the key of C using only two of its three chords, C and G7. We must now learn the third chord of the key of C, the F chord.

STEP ONE: Look at the sketch and the chord diagram given in Figures 61 and 62. The first and second

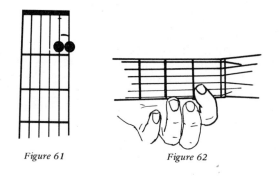

Figure 61   *Figure 62*

strings are to be fretted at the first fret. The curved line connecting the dots on the chord diagram representing fingers means that both of the strings are to be fretted by one finger. This can be seen in Figure 62. With the "flat" or the "side" of the index finger, fret the first *and* second strings at the first fret. You will probably have to push harder for those two notes than for any of the previous notes we have attempted. This is because we are holding down two strings with one finger. Sound the first and second strings. They should sound as good as the first string fretted at the first fret in the G7 chord or the second string fretted at the first fret in the C chord. As soon as you can hold down both strings and make them sound good, go on to the next step without moving your hand.

STEP TWO: Without moving the index finger, use the second finger to fret the third string at the second fret with the tip of the finger as shown in Figures 63 and 64. Now play the first three strings to see if they

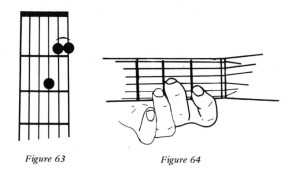

Figure 63   *Figure 64*

all sound good. If the third string sounds good but the first or second strings sound bad, you moved the index finger while putting the second finger down. Go back to step one and proceed to step two without moving the index finger. If the first two strings sound good, but the third string is bad, move the second finger to find the right position, but be careful not to move the index finger out of position.

STEP THREE: When the first three strings sound good simultaneously, use the third finger to fret the fourth string at the third fret, completing the F chord as seen in Figures 65 and 66. If you find that the base

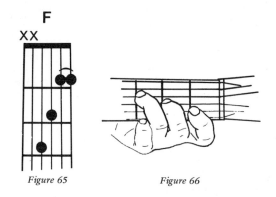

Figure 65   *Figure 66*

of the third finger is inadvertently touching and deadening the first string while fretting the fourth string, try moving the elbow (of your left arm) closer to your body. This will make your fingers arch over the strings.

Repeat the three steps above until the F chord can be played with moderate proficiency.

Questions:

1—How many fingers are used in this F chord? _____
2—How many strings are covered? _____
3—How is this done? _____

_____

4—How many chords in a key? _____

5—What are the chords in the key of C? _____
_____

6—Which fret does the index finger play in the G7 chord? _____

7—Which finger is used on the first fret in the F chord? _____

8—What does the third finger do when changing from C to F? _____

9—How many strings are sounded in this F chord? _____

10—Which strings are *not* sounded in this F chord? _____

11—What does the second finger do when changing from the F chord to the C chord? _____
_____

12—What are the three steps in learning the F chord?
_____
_____
_____

13—Which fingers change frets when changing from the G7 chord to the F chord? _____

14—Which fingers change frets when changing from the F chord to the C chord? _____

15—What must the index finger do when changing from the F chord to the C chord? _____

16—What does the index finger do when changing from the F chord to the G7 chord? _____
_____

This song should be an easy beginning in learning how to use the F chord. Only two measures of F chord appear and no left hand work is required during these two measures. Be sure to take the song slow enough so that the chord changes are smooth.

Oh, Susanna - Solo

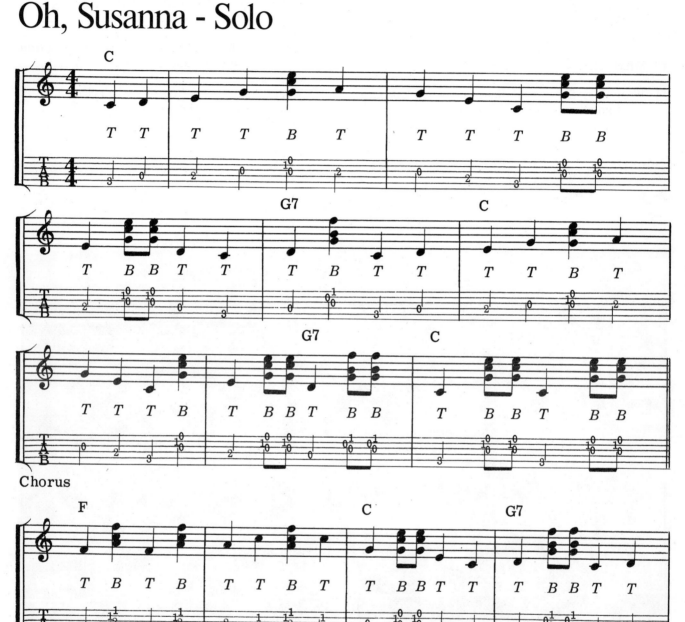

Chorus

In this solo we use the F chord with double brushes and we also use the fifth string open while holding the F chord.

Banks of the Ohio - Melody

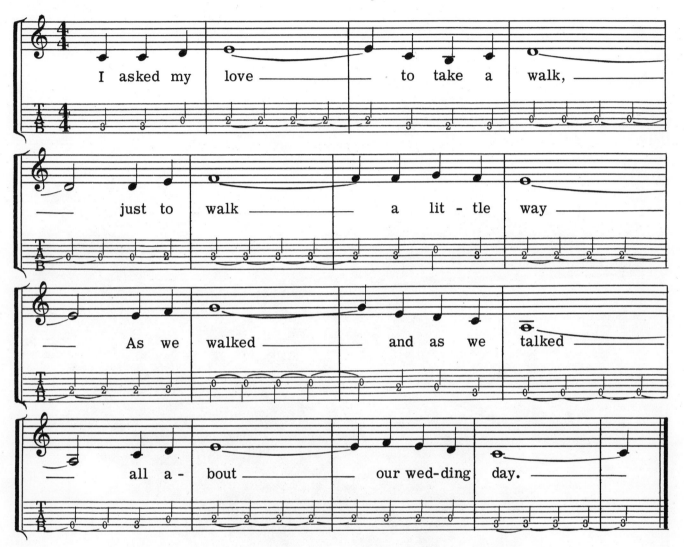

I asked my love to take a walk,
just to walk a little way
As we walked and as we talked
all about our wedding day.

C   G7
I asked my love to take a walk,

                    C
Just to walk a little way,

                                F
And as we walked and as we talked

          C   G7   C
All about our wedding day.

CHORUS:
Only say that you'll be mine,
In my arms will happy be.
Down beside where the waters flow,
By the banks of the Ohio.

I took her by her lily-white hand,
Dragged her down to the river strand.
Pushed her in and let her drown,
Stood and watched as she floated down.

Was coming home 'tween twelve and one,
Thinking of the deed I'd done.
I murdered the only girl I love
Because she would not marry me.

The very next morn, about half past four,
The sheriff's men knocked at my door,
"Now, young man, let's come and go
Down to the banks of the Ohio."

Questions:

17—What is the rhythm of the twelfth measure? _____
_____

18—The thirteenth measure? _____
_____

19—Which finger should be used to fret the third note of the thirteenth measure? _____

Recommended Listening:

Pete Seeger, *American Favorite Ballads, Volume 4*, Folkways FA 2323.
New Lost City Ramblers — Volume 2, Folkways FA 2397.
Native American Ballads, RCA Victor LPV-548.

Banks of the Ohio - Solo

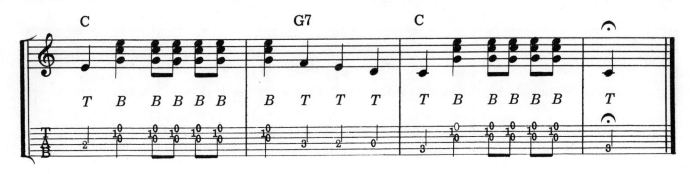

This song should require little introduction if the student has mastered the previous material. *John Hardy* will give a little extra practice in using the F chord in Carter picking. Notice that the little finger should be used to fret the third string at the third fret in the third measure.

John Hardy - Melody

John   Har - dy, he   was   a   des-p'rate_   lit - tle_

man,_   He   car - ried two   guns   ev - 'ry   day_

_   He   shot   down a   man   on the   West Vir - gin-ia_

line,   you ought a   seen John   Har - dy get-tin' a - way, Poor

Boy,   ought to   seen John   Har - dy gettin' a - way.

C   F   C
John Hardy, he was a desp'rate little man.

  F   C
He carried two guns ev'ry day.

  F   C
He shot down a man on the West Virginia Line.

                    G7   C
And you ought to seen John Hardy gettin' away,

    poor boy,

            G7
You ought to seen John Hardy gettin' away.

John Hardy, he got to the East Stone bridge,
He thought that he would be free,
And it's up steps the man and took him by his arm,
Says, "Johnny, come along with me." (2)

He sent for his poppy and his mommy, too,
To come and go his bail,
But there ain't no bail for a murderin' man,
So they threw John Hardy back in jail. (2)

John Hardy had a pretty little girl,
The dress that she wore was blue,

As she come a-skipping through the old jail house,
Sayin', "Poppa, I've been true to you." (2)

John Hardy had another little girl,
The dress that she wore was red:
She followed John Hardy to his hangin' ground,
Says, "Poppy, I'd rather be dead." (2)

John Hardy was felled on his scaffold high,
With his loving wife by his side,
And the last words they heard him say,
"I'll meet you in that sweet by and by." (2)

"I've been to the east and I've been to the west,
I've been the wide world 'round.
I been to the river and I been baptized,
And now I'm on my hangin' ground." (2)

Recommended Listening:

    Pete Seeger Sings American Ballads, Folkways FA
      2319.
    Carter Family — *Anthology of American Folk
      Music,* Folkways FA 2195.

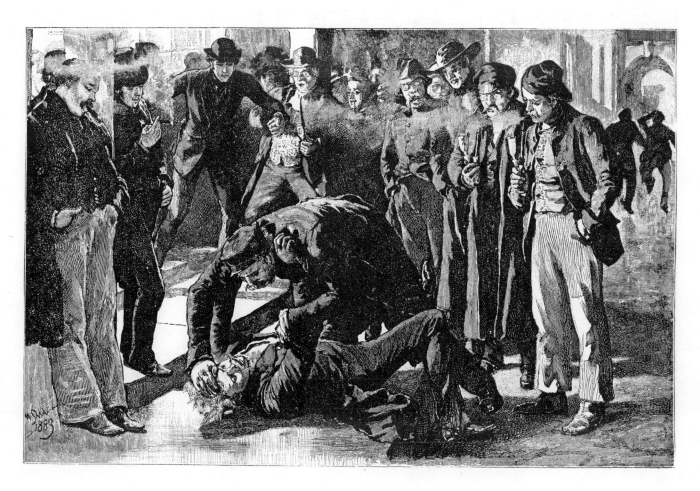

John Hardy - Solo

WILDWOOD FLOWER — REPEATS

In this song we introduce a new musical notation that is used very commonly to indicate that one portion of the music is to be played twice. These are called *repeat marks* and are illustrated in Figure 67.

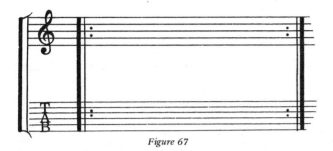

Figure 67

The repeat marks are two vertical double bar lines preceded by two dots. All of the music enclosed by the repeat marks is to be played twice in succession.

Notice that in the melody to *Wildwood Flower* measures one through four have exactly the same notes and timing as measures five through eight. Thus, in the solo version of *Wildwood Flower*, the measures corresponding to the repeated portions of the melody are enclosed in the repeat marks at the beginning of the second measure and at the end of the sixth measure. When we play the solo we play up to and including the sixth measure as we would if there were no repeat marks. Then, instead of playing the seventh measure, we go back and play the *second measure again*. We then continue playing the repeated portion (the second, third, fourth, fifth and sixth measures) and, at the second repeat mark, we continue to play the seventh measure. In this way the second through sixth measures have been played twice in succession. (If only one double bar with the dots pointing toward the beginning of the music were included, the repeat would include all the material before the repeat mark up to the beginning of the piece.)

Wildwood Flower - Melody

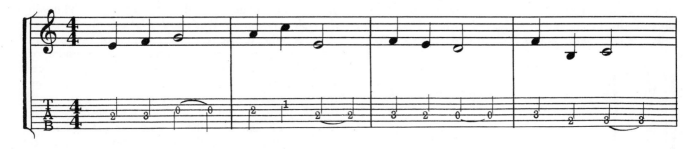

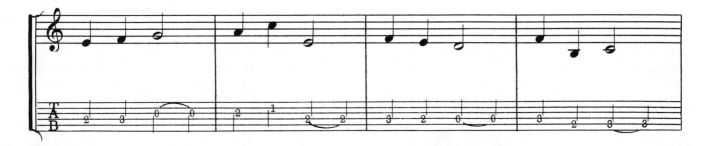

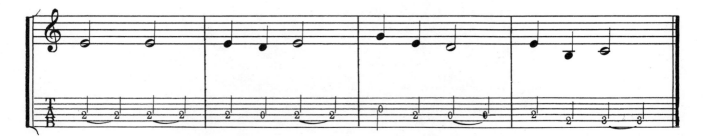

Questions:

20—Which finger should be used to play the second note of the second measure? _____

21—Which finger for the first note of the third measure? _____

22—For the first note of the fifth measure? _____

23—For the second note of the fifth measure? _____

24—Which for the second note of the eighth measure? _____

25—How are repeat marks indicated? _____

26—How many measures are repeated in this song? _____

Recommended Listening:

Carter Family — *Famous*, Harmony HL-7280 ($1.98).

Carter Family — *Original and Great*, RCA Camden CAL-586 ($1.98).

American Banjo Scruggs Style, Folkways FA 2314.

Wildwood Flower - Solo

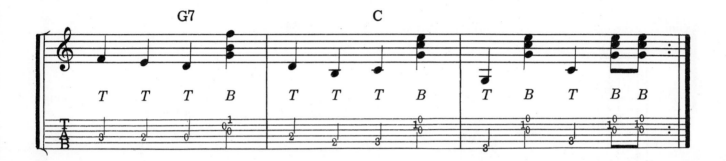

Figures 68 and 69 show the old F chord which we already know. We will call this the "four-string F

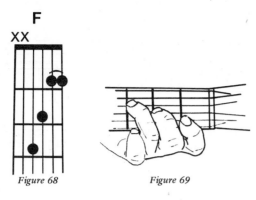

Figure 68   Figure 69

chord" since only four of the six strings of the guitar

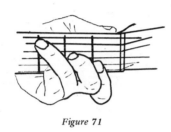

Figure 70   Figure 71

are fretted. The next step in learning our new F chord is to move the third finger from the fourth string, third fret to the fifth string, third fret. This is illustrated in Figures 70 and 71. Now, to fill the vacancy on the fourth string we use the little finger. The new F chord, which is called the five-string F chord, is shown in Figures 72 and 73.

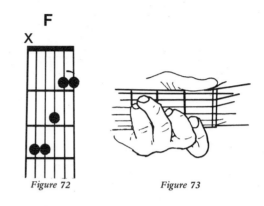

Figure 72   Figure 73

You should use the five-string F chord in playing the solo to *Worried Man Blues* below.

Worried Man Blues - Melody

C
It takes a worried man to sing a worried song,
F   C
It takes a worried man to sing a worried song.

It takes a worried man to sing a worried song,
          G7   C
I'm worried now, but I won't be worried long.

I went across the river, and I lay down to sleep. (3)
When I woke up, I had shackles on my feet.

Twenty-nine links of chain around my leg. (3)
And on each link, an initial of my name.

I asked the judge, what might be my fine? (3)
Twenty-one years on the Rocky Mountain Line.

The train arrived, twenty coaches long. (3)
The girl I love is on that train and gone.

I looked down the track as far as I could see. (3)
Little bitty hand was a-wavin' after me.

If anyone should ask you, who composed this song, (3)
Tell him it was me, and I sing it all day long.

Questions:

27—Which finger is used for the five-string F chord that wasn't used in the four-string F chord? _____

28—Which finger is used to fret the fifth string in the five-string F chord? _____

29—In *Worried Man Blues*, which F chord is used in the fifth measure? _____

30—In the sixth measure? _____

31—Which finger is used to play the last note of the fifth measure? _____

32—Which for the third beat of the twelfth measure? _____

33—How many out of the chord notes are in this song?

Recommended Listening:

Carter Family — *Famous,* Harmony HL 7280 ($1.98).

Carter Family — *Smokey Mountain Ballads,* RCA Victor LPV-507.

Woody Guthrie — Library of Congress, Elektra EKL-271/2.

Pete Seeger — *At The Village Gate,* Folkways FA 2450.

CHORD ANALYSIS BOX—WORRIED MAN BLUES

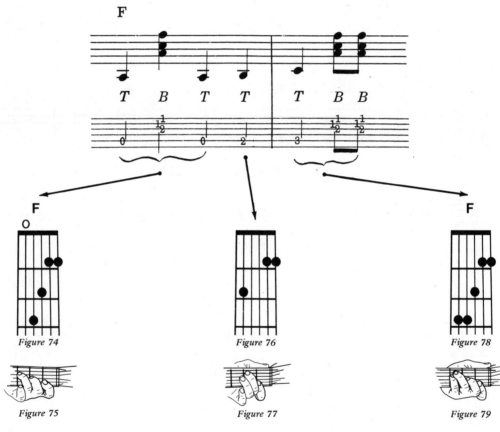

Figure 74

Figure 76

Figure 78

Figure 75

Figure 77

Figure 79

Worried Man Blues - Solo

We can now add the use of F chords to our study of waltz time. *Danville Girl* can be easily played with only the four-string F chords.

Danville Girl - Melody

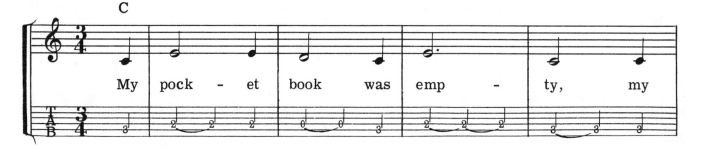

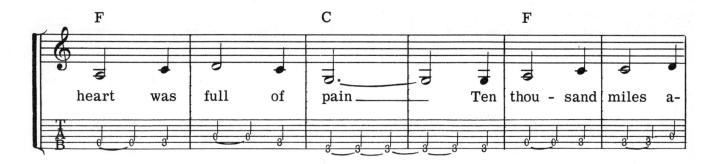

C
My pocket book was empty,

     F   C
My heart was full of pain;

     F   C
Ten thousand miles away from home,
 G7   C
Bummin' a railroad train.

I was standing on the platform,
Smoking a big cigar,
Waiting for the next freight train
To carry an empty car.

I stopped me off at Danville,
Got stuck on a Danville girl.
You can bet your life she was out of sight,
She wore those Danville curls.

She took me to her parlor,
Treated me nice and fine.
She got me out of the notion
To go bummin' all the time.

She wore her hat on the back of her head,
Like them high-tone people do.
But the very next train come down the line,
I bid that girl adieu.

Danville Girl - Solo

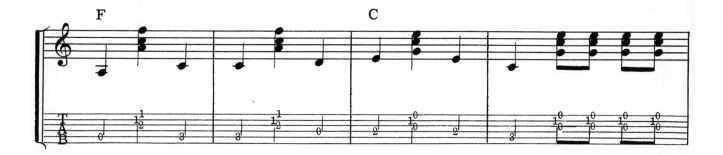

Carefully compare the melody line of this song with the melody of the solo. You will find that many rhythmic complications have been inserted. It seems as if the thumb-brush-brush pattern has been re-estab-

lished, but on the wrong beat. A tremendous amount of rhythmic interest can be generated in this way.

The new material for the left hand is explained in the CHORD ANALYSIS BOX.

Lone Green Valley - Melody

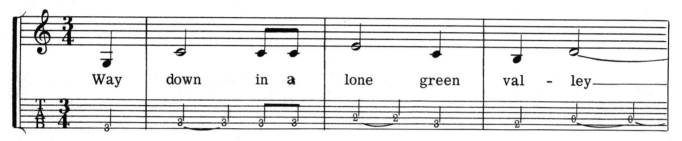

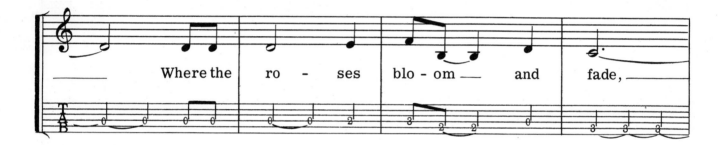

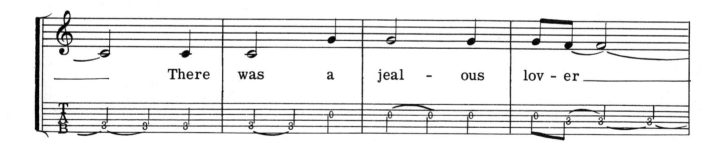

C   G7
Way down in the lone green valley,
                              C
Where the roses bloom and fade,
                    F
There was a jealous lover
   G7   C
In love with a beautiful maid.

One night the moon shone brightly,
The stars were shining, too,
And to this maiden's cottage
The jealous lover drew.

"Come love, and we will wander,
Where the woods are gay,
While walking we will ponder
All about our wedding day."

So on and on they wandered,
The night birds sang above,
The jealous lover grew angry
With the beautiful girl he loved.

Down on her knees before him
She pleaded for her life;
But deep into her bosom
He plunged that fatal knife.

"Oh, Willie, won't you tell me
Why you have taken my life?
You know I've always loved you
And wanted to be your wife.

"I never have deceived you,
But with my dying breath,
I will forgive you, Willie,
And close my eyes in death."

CHORD ANALYSIS BOX—LONE GREEN VALLEY

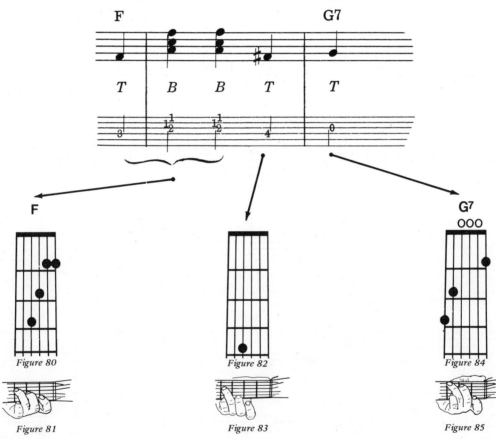

Figure 80

Figure 81

Figure 82

Figure 83

Figure 84

Figure 85

Lone Green Valley - Solo

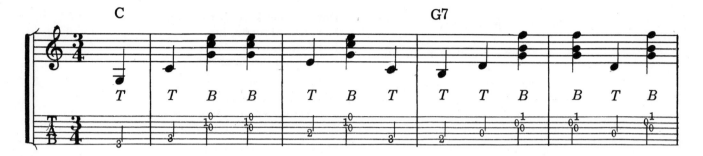

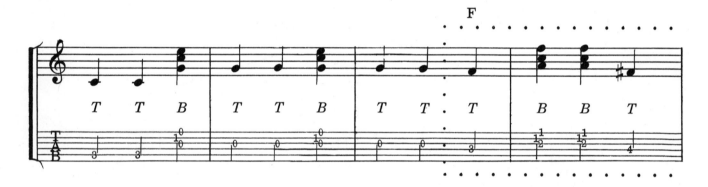

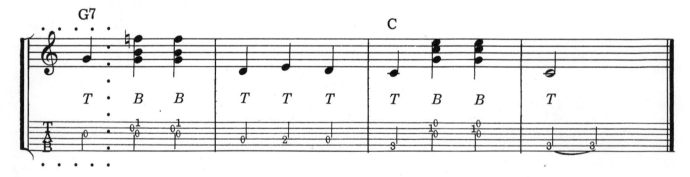

ANSWERS TO QUESTIONS

1—Three fingers.
2—Four strings.
3—Index finger covers two strings.
4—Three chords.
5—C, F, and G7.
6—First fret.
7—Index finger.
8—Change string only.
9—Four strings.
10—Fifth and sixth strings.
11—Change strings only.
12—See text.
13—None.
14—None.
15—Release first string.
16—Release second string.
17—1, 2, 3, &, 4, &.

18—1, 2, &, 3, 4.
19—Third finger.
20—Little finger.
21—Second finger.
22—Second finger.
23—Second finger.
24—Little finger.
25—See text.
26—Five measures.
27—Little finger.
28—Third finger.
29—Four-string F chord.
30—Five-string F chord.
31—Second finger.
32—Little finger.
33—15.

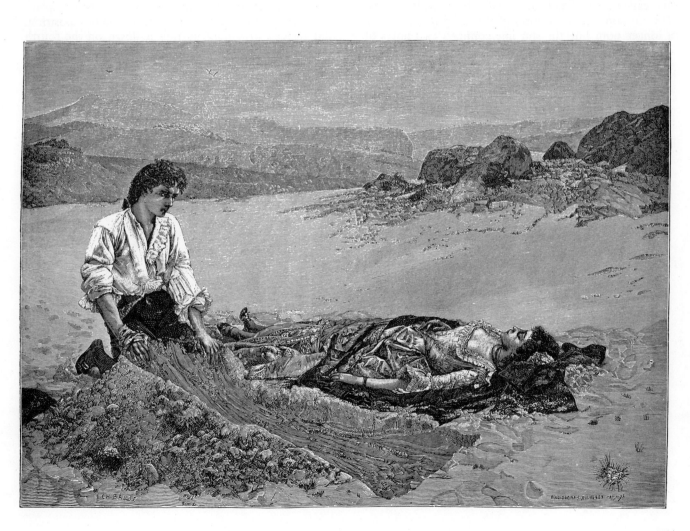

ADVANCED CARTER STYLES

TOM DOOLEY — THE HAMMER

In this chapter we will learn several methods of embellishing melody in the Carter style. These will be some additional techniques for the left hand. The first method of embellishment that we will consider is called the *hammer*.

The hammer is a note that is made to sound, not by the right hand, but by the *left hand*. With a little experimentation, you will find that you can sound the strings of the guitar by simply hitting them with the tips of the fingers of the left hand. You may have noticed this when you "grabbed" a chord a little too hard. This, basically, is the method of the hammer. One "hammers" the strings by bringing the fingers of the left hand down on the string hard enough to make the string sound as it strikes the fret. More sound can be obtained if the string is first sounded by the right hand in the normal fashion and then hammered by the left hand.

The hammer in the tablature is indicated by the letter "H" as shown in Figure 102. It usually consists of two eighth notes which are connected by a curved line called a *slur line* (not to be confused with the tie). The tie connects two notes of the same pitch making a longer note but the slur line connects two notes of different pitch, both of which are sounded. The hammer almost always starts on an open string, therefore

one must first decide which finger to lift. One then sounds the open note. The finger is then hammered down on the fingerboard of the guitar so that the second note of the pair is sounded.

Let us now play the tablature given in Figure 102.

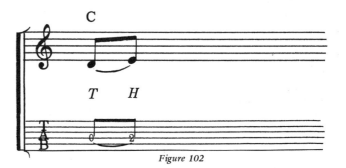

Figure 102

Hold down the C chord as shown. Now lift the second finger of the left hand so that the fourth string is open. With the thumb of the right hand sound the fourth string open as indicated in the tablature. Now replace the second finger into the normal C chord position. But instead of simply putting it down on the fourth string at the second fret, hammer it down so that the second note sounds out. This should be practiced until

the second note is clear and almost as loud as the first note of the pair. The rhythm of this figure is the same as the rhythm of the double brush, i.e., two eighth notes.

Questions:

1—The hammered note is sounded by the _____ hand.

2—The note preceding the hammered note is sounded by the _____ hand.

3—Rhythmically, the hammered figure consists of two _____ notes.

4—This is equal in time value to one _____ note.

5—Why does one lift fingers of the left hand for the hammer? _____ _____

6—The hammer is indicated by the letter _____.

7—What other indication is found in the tablature and music for the hammer? _____

8—In the first measure of *Tom Dooley*, which beat contains the hammer? _____

9—Which string is sounded open? _____

10—Which string is hammered? _____

11—At which fret is the hammered note sounded? _____

12—Which finger must be lifted for this hammer? _____

13—How many different hammers are in this song? _____

14—What is the count for two eighth notes? _____

15—Count the second measure of *Tom Dooley:* _____

16—Count the first measure: _____

17—The fifth measure: _____

18—The seventh measure: _____

19—Fill out the table for each hammer.

	Chord	String	Finger	Open note in chord?
a.—	C			
b.—		fifth		no
c.—			2nd	

Tom Dooley - Solo

GOSPEL SHIP — MORE HAMMERS

In this song we hammer on a note out of the C chord on the third string. Notice that if we leave the second finger down on the third string at the second fret during the following brushes a distinctly different sound is obtained than if we return it to the original position of the normal C chord. The choice is up to the student, but you should practice so you can play this figure both ways.

Recommended Listening:

Carter Family — *Famous*, Harmony HL 7280 ($1.98).

Gospel Ship - Solo

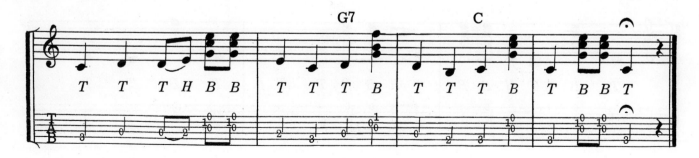

WORRIED MAN BLUES —
MORE HAMMERED NOTES

This song has been arranged to include several new hammered notes. You should compare it carefully to the version given in Chapter 3.

Recommended Listening:

Carter Family — *Famous,* Harmony HL 7280.

Carter Family — *Smokey Mountain Ballads,* RCA Victor LPV-507.

Woody Guthrie — Library of Congress, Elektra EKL-271/2.

Pete Seeger — *At The Village Gate,* Folkways FA 2450.

Worried Man Blues - Solo

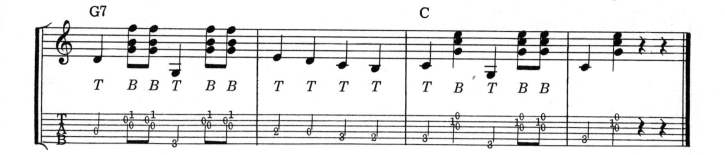

GO TELL AUNT RHODY — PICKED NOTES

The second form of embellishment that we will study is called by many names, the pick, pick-off, pull-off, but we'll simply call it the *picked note* and it will be symbolized in the tablature by the letter "P" as shown in Figure 103. The picked note is also sounded by the left hand but quite differently from the

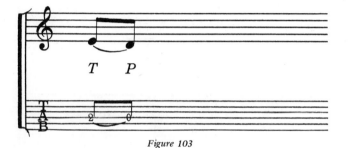

Figure 103

hammer. The picked note is *plucked* by a finger of the left hand. Let's play the figure in the tablature above. Sound the fourth string of a normal C chord. Then, while the note is still sounding, remove the second finger of the left hand from the fingerboard of the guitar by pulling that second finger into your hand and in the process it will pluck the fourth string causing it to sound open. Practice this until it can be done smoothly. The picked note starts with a fretted string which is sounded by the right hand and is completed by an open string sounded by the left hand. The rhythm of the pick is the same as that of the hammer; i.e., two eighth notes.

Questions:

20—How many picked figures are in *Go Tell Aunt Rhody* below? _____

21—What is the rhythm of the first measure? _____ _____

22—The picked figure consists of _____ eighth notes.

23—Which finger is used to sound the picked note in the first measure? _____

24—Is the picked note "in the chord"? _____

25—Is the picked note in the melody? _____

26—What does H mean in tablature? _____ _____

27—Must all starting notes for the pick figure be in the chord? _____

28—Which finger plays the first note of the fourth measure? _____

29—How is the second note of the fourth measure sounded? _____

30—Is the first note of the fourth measure in the chord? _____

31—Is the picked note "in the chord" in the fourth measure? _____

32—A pick is symbolized by a _____ and a _____.

33—In what way is the pick a reverse of the hammer? _____

34—What does each letter used in tablature mean, T, B, H, P? _____

Go Tell Aunt Rhody - Solo

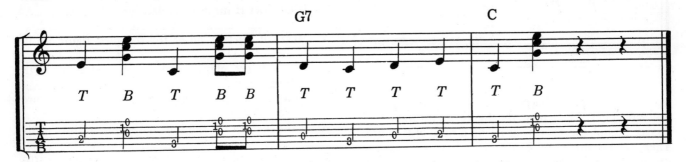

**GO TELL AUNT RHODY —
COMBINED HAMMERS AND PICKS**

Questions:

36—How many different hammers and picks are in
 this song? _____

37—Which finger should be used for the hammer in
 the third measure (*not* the third finger)? _____

38—Which finger is used to fret the last note of the
 fifth measure? _____

39—Complete this table:

Measure	1	3	4	5	6
Beat					
Hammer or Pick					
String					
Finger Used					
Is 1st note in chord?					
Is 2nd note in chord?					

Go Tell Aunt Rhody - Solo

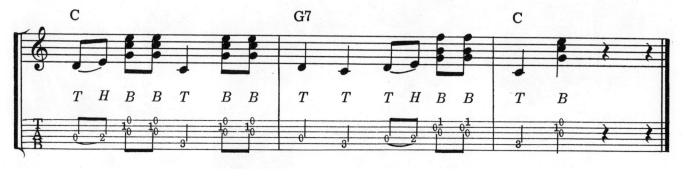

JOHN HARDY — MORE HAMMERS

A slightly different form of hammer is introduced in this song. In the seventh measure, we find that a hammer is required to go *from* a fretted note *to* a fret- ted note. This will not be difficult if you hold the four-string F chord and use the little finger for the hammer.

John Hardy - Solo

OLD JOE CLARK — PICKS

In this song we introduce a pick that goes from a fretted string to a fretted string instead of to an open string. In the first measure remember to use the second finger for the hammer as shown in Figures 106 and 107 and the little finger for the pick as in Figures 110 and 111. Notice that both the second finger and the third finger must be fretting the same string in Figures 108 and 109 so that the second fret will sound after the pick as in Figures 110 and 111. Remember to distinguish carefully between a double brush (two eighth notes) and two brushes (two quarter notes) as in the fourth measure.

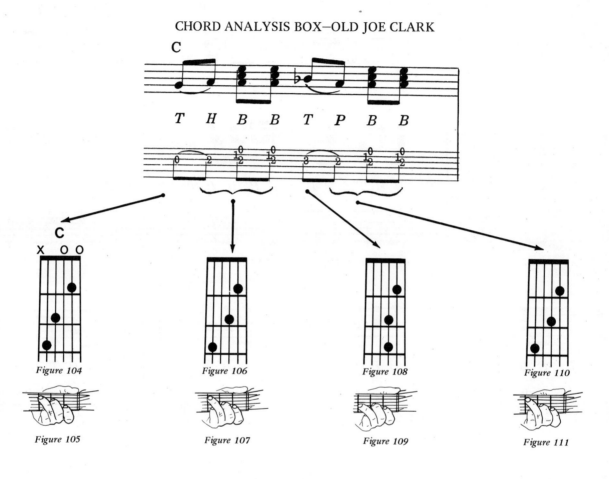

CHORD ANALYSIS BOX—OLD JOE CLARK

Figure 104

Figure 105

Figure 106

Figure 107

Figure 108

Figure 109

Figure 110

Figure 111

Recommended Listening:

New Lost City Ramblers — Volume 5, Folkways FA 2395.

Traditional Music at Newport—1964, Pt 2, Van-guard VSD-79183.

Washboard Band, Folkways FA 2201.

Woody Guthrie — Library of Congress, Elektra EKL-271/2.

George Pegram and Walter Parham — *Pickin' and Blowin'*, Riverside RLP 12-650.

Wade Ward — *Banjo Songs From The Southern Mountains*, Prestige 25004.

Old Joe Clark - Solo

Here are the melody and a simple arrangement of a favorite cowboy song that should give no difficulty.

Questions:

40—How many different rhythmic patterns are found in this song? _____

41—Count the fourth measure: _____
42—Count the twelfth measure: _____

Recommended Listening:

Pete Seeger — *American Favorite Ballads*, Folkways FA 2030.

I Ride An Old Paint - Melody

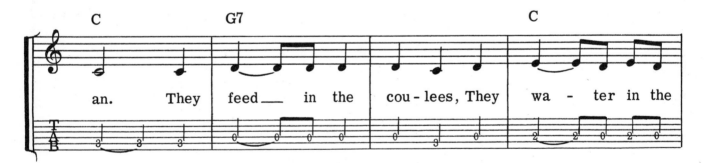

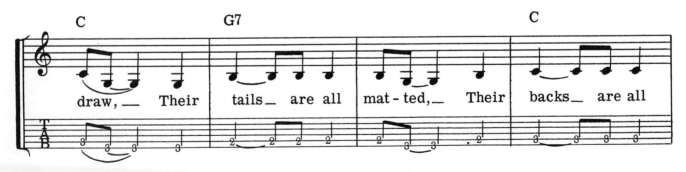

Chorus

raw, Ride a- round lit-tle do-gies, Ride a- round them

slow, For the Fi - ery and snuf-fy are ra- rin' to go.

C
I ride an old paint,

I lead an old Dan.
    G7
I'm goin' to Montan'
    C
For to throw the hoolian.
G7
They feed in the coulees,
    C
They water in the draw,
    G7
Their tails are all matted,
    C
Their backs are all raw.

CHORUS:
    G7
Ride around little dogies,
    C
Ride around them slow,
    G7
For the fiery and snuffy
    C
Are rarin' to go.

Old Bill Jones
Had two daughters and a son.
The son went to college
And the daughters went wrong.
His wife was killed
In a poolroom fight,
Still he keeps singin'
From morning 'til night.

Oh, when I die,
Take my saddle from the wall,
Put it on my pony
And lead him from the stall.
Tie my bones to his back,
Turn our faces to the West,
And we'll ride the prairies
That we love the best:

I Ride An Old Paint - Solo

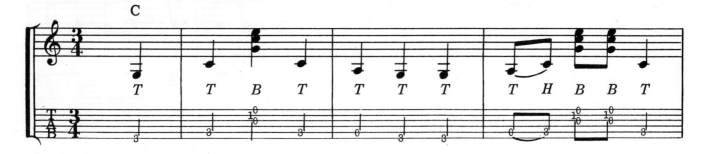

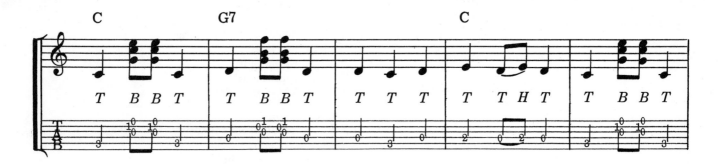

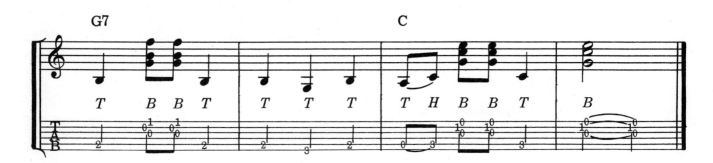

DANVILLE GIRL — MORE WALTZ TIME

This song presents a little more complicated use of hammers and picks in waltz time. The use of the hammers in the F chords will probably present the most difficulty. The first F chord is examined in the CHORD ANALYSIS BOX. The use of the chord positions in the second F chord is very similar.

Recommended Listening:

Jack Elliot, Archives of Folk Music 210.
Jack Elliot — *Ramblin'*, Reprise 6284.

CHORD ANALYSIS BOX—DANVILLE GIRL

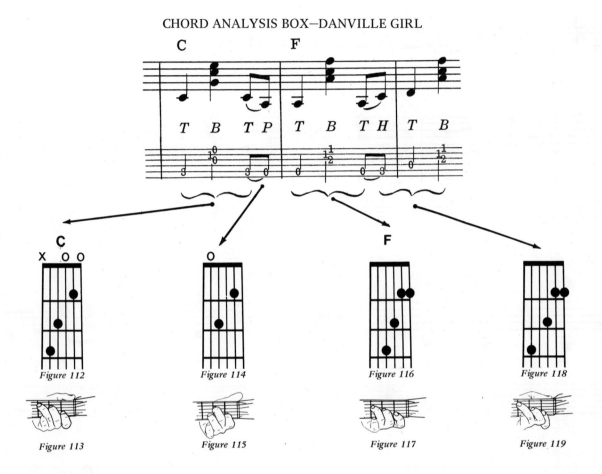

Figure 112

Figure 113

Figure 114

Figure 115

Figure 116

Figure 117

Figure 118

Figure 119

Danville Girl - Solo

WORRIED MAN BLUES — MORE USE OF HAMMERS AND PICKS

This song contains more practice in the use of hammers and picks in various chords and with various fingers. Be especially careful to work out the hammers in the F chords illustrated in the CHORD ANALYSIS BOX so they are clean. Also be sure to compare this arrangement of *Worried Man Blues* to the previous arrangements and see how and where the hammers and picks are used to embellish the melody.

Recommended Listening:

Carter Family — *Famous*, Harmony HL 7280 ($1.98).
Carter Family — *Smokey Mountain Ballads*, RCA Victor LPV-507.
Woody Guthrie — Library of Congress, Elektra EKL-271/2.
Pete Seeger — *At the Village Gate*, Folkways FA 2450.

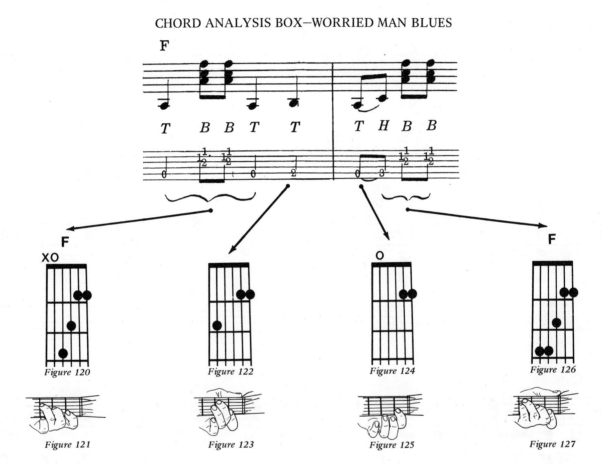

CHORD ANALYSIS BOX—WORRIED MAN BLUES

Figure 120

Figure 121

Figure 122

Figure 123

Figure 124

Figure 125

Figure 126

Figure 127

Worried Man Blues - Solo

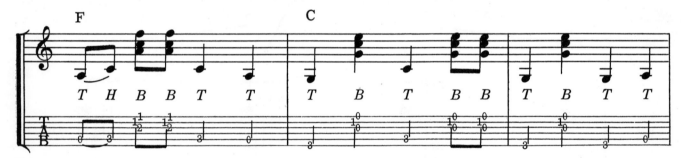

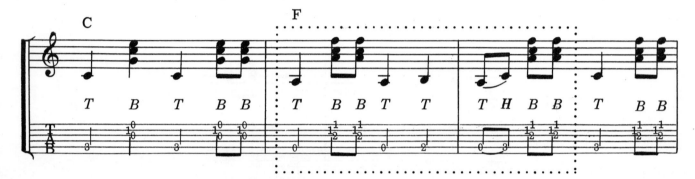

WILDWOOD FLOWER — INDEX FINGER NOTES

This version of *Wildwood Flower* contains, in addition to hammers and picks, some notes to be sounded by the index finger of the right hand. The correct finger position before and after picking the second string is shown in Figures 128 and 129, respectively.

Figure 128

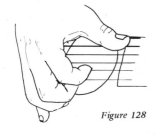

Figure 129

The places where the index finger is to be used are indicated by the letter "I" in the music and tablature.

In the fifth measure, just before changing to the C chord, the index finger plays the second string open. Notice that the rhythm of the "thumb-index" figure is exactly the same as the rhythm of a "thumb-hammer" or a "thumb-pick" figure; i.e., two eighth notes. The fifth measure would be counted: 1, &, 2, &, 3, 4, &.

The measure following the repeat mark is by far the most difficult of the song. The first beat is a thumb note and the second beat is a brush. This much should give no difficulty. The third beat is a thumb note to be played on the *first string*. The last beat consists of two eighth notes, the first corresponding to a thumb note on the third string and the second eighth note to an index finger note on the second string. The next measure begins with a thumb note sounding the first string open again. This should prove conquerable with a little practice.

Wildwood Flower - Solo

WABASH CANNON BALL — A NEW F CHORD

This is the last and most complex song of this chapter and should serve as a good review for all the techniques that we have learned. In addition, we will have to learn how to fret the sixth string of the guitar with the thumb to play *Wabash Cannon Ball.*

The use of the thumb, especially in the F chord, is very common among folk guitarists both traditional and city bred. It is not a very difficult procedure. To begin, you must realize that to fret the strings with the thumb is vastly different from fretting with the fingers. With the finger, we *push* the strings down to

position as is shown in Figure 130. Allow the thumb to come up over the sixth string at the first fret as shown in Figure 131. Now, do not attempt to fret the sixth string by pushing down on it with the thumb, instead push the thumb into the guitar as if you were squeezing the guitar neck. Now pull the thumb down toward your elbow. By this type of motion, you can have the fleshy part of your thumb over the sixth string and pull it down hard enough to fret the string properly as illustrated in Figure 132. This will probably take some practice, so have patience.

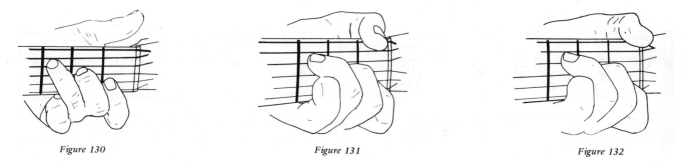

Figure 130   Figure 131   Figure 132

the frets, when we use the thumb we will *pull* the strings down to the fret.

Try the following procedure: Play the four-string F chord that we already know. Let the neck of the guitar sink deep into the palm of your hand so that the fretting fingers are pushing the guitar into your hand in the direction of your wrist. Your thumb should be fairly free to wiggle around without losing the chord

Make sure you learn the melody line of the song before attempting the solo. Otherwise the solo will not make much sense. The amount of ornamentation used in the solo is extreme but still very tasteful.

The most difficult portion of the solo to *Wabash Cannon Ball* has been analyzed in a CHORD ANALYSIS BOX. Notice the use of the thumb in the F chords in Figures 141 through 146.

Wabash Cannon Ball - Melody

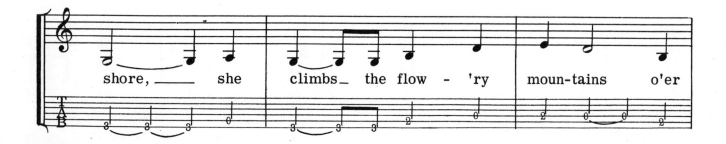

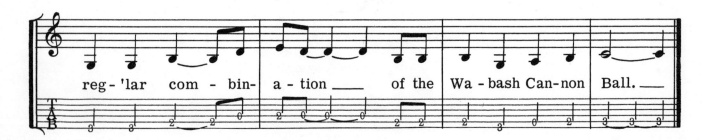

C   F
Out from the wide Pacific to the broad Atlantic shore

 G7
She climbs the flow'ry mountain o'er hills and by

   C
the shore.

            F
Although she's tall and handsome and she's known

 full well by all,

   G7   C
She's a reg'lar combination of the Wabash Cannon Ball.

Oh, the eastern states are dandy, so the western
  people say:
Chicago, and Rock Island, St. Louis by the way.
To the lakes of Minnesota where the rippling waters
  fall,
No changes to be taken on the Wabash Cannon Ball.

CHORUS:
Oh, listen to the jingle, the rumble and the roar,
As she glides along the woodlands, o'er hills and
  by the shore,
As she climbs the flow'ry mountains hear the merry
  hobo squall,
She glides along the woodland, the Wabash Cannon
  Ball.

Oh, here's to Daddy Cleaton, let his name forever be;
And long be remembered in the courts of Tennessee.
For he is a good old rounder 'till the curtain 'round
  him falls,
He'll be carried back to victory on the Wabash Cannon
  Ball.

I have rode the I. C. Limited, also the Royal Blue,
Across the eastern countries on Elkhorn Number Two.
I have rode those highball trains from coast to coast,
  that's all —
But I have found no equal to the Wabash Cannon Ball.

Recommended Listening:

 Carter Family — *Original and Great,* RCA Camden
  CAL-586 ($1.98).
 Pete Seeger — *American Favorite Ballads,* Folkways
  FA 2030.
 Doc Watson — *Doc and Jean at Folk City,* Folk-
  ways FA 2426.

CHORD ANALYSIS BOX—WABASH CANNON BALL

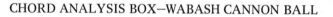

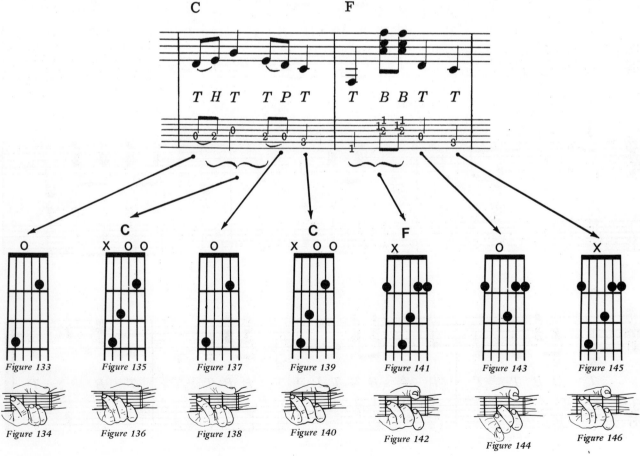

Figure 133 Figure 135 Figure 137 Figure 139 Figure 141 Figure 143 Figure 145

Figure 134 Figure 136 Figure 138 Figure 140 Figure 142 Figure 144 Figure 146

Wabash Cannon Ball - Solo

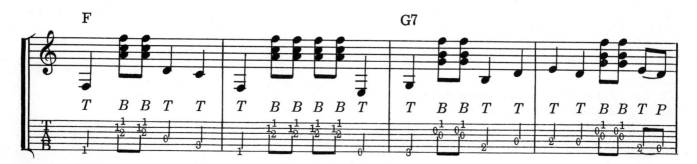

ANSWERS TO QUESTIONS

[Again, for all unanswered questions, it's up to you.]

1—Left hand.
2—Right hand thumb.
3—Eighth notes.
4—Quarter.
5—
6—H.
7—Slur line.
8—Third beat.
9—Fifth string.
10—Fifth string.
11—Third fret.
12—Third finger.
13—Three hammers.
14—1, &.
15—1, 2, &, 3, 4, &.
16—1, 2, 3, &, 4, &.
17—1, 2, 3, &, 4.
18—1, &, 2, &, 3, 4.
19—a—C chord, fifth string, third finger, open note out of chord.

b—G7, fifth string, second finger, yes.
c—G7, fourth string, second finger, open note in chord.
20—Two, both same.
21—1, 2, &, 3, &, 4, &.
22—Two.
23—Second finger.
24—No.
25—Yes.
26—Hammer.
27—No.
28—Second finger.
29—Pick.
30—No.
31—Yes.
32—P and slur line.
36—Five.
37—Little finger.
38—Little finger.
39—See table below
40—Four.
41—1, &, 2, &, 3.
42—1, 2, &, 3.

Measure	1	3	4	5	6
Beat	3rd	3rd	1st	1st	3rd
Hammer or Pick	P	H	P	H	H
String	4th	4th	4th	4th	4th
Finger Used	2nd	4th	2nd	2nd	2nd
Is 1st note in chord?	yes	yes	no	no	yes
Is 2nd note in chord?	no	no	yes	yes	no

BEGINNING FINGERPICKING

INTRODUCTION

We have now completed our basic study of Carter style solos. We can now go on to the second major guitar solo style. In the broadest sense, it should be called "fingerstyle" guitar since various combinations of fingers are used simultaneously and independently to carry several voices on the guitar. This will become obvious by the end of this chapter. The particular style we will begin studying is most commonly called "fingerpicking." This may be differentiated from "bluepicking" (a form of fingerpicking often associated with blues, though it is not as free, rhythmically) which employs almost the same techniques but on a different rhythmic basis. Both fingerpicking and bluespicking use a constantly sounded bass pattern. Other styles of fingerpicking and bluespicking do not use a constant bass and for more information on these styles the interested student should consult Stephan Grossman's *Country Blues Guitar.* I will attempt not to duplicate the material presented in that book, but I hope the current book will provide a background that will be useful to the study of that and other books.

Fingerpicking is a guitar style where the melody is played by the fingers on the higher pitched string and the thumb is used to accompany the melody in some way on the bass strings. Notice that this is exactly the reverse of the Carter picking style where the melody was played in the bass strings. For the present we will restrict ourselves to playing the melody with the index finger of the right hand and accompanying it with an alternating pattern played by the thumb.

For the first few songs we will use only two right hand figures. The first is simply a thumb note indicated by T in the tablature. This is no different than in Carter picking and should cause no problems.

The second right hand figure is one of the most basic in all fingerpicking. It is the simultaneous sounding of two strings, one by the index finger and one by the thumb. The correct right hand position for this figure, called the *pinch,* is shown in Figure 147 and is indicated in the tablature by $\frac{I}{T}$. This means that the index finger plays the top note of the pair and the thumb plays the bottom note at the same time.

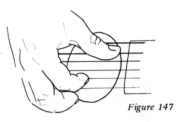

Figure 147

TOM DOOLEY — FIRST FINGERPICKING TUNE

For the first few songs in fingerpicking we will use melodies with which we are already familiar, like *Tom Dooley.* Look at the melody given below. Notice that it is different from the melody given in the first chapter of this book. It is now to be played on the first, second and third strings of the guitar rather than on the fourth, fifth, and sixth strings. When you play this melody to become familiar with where the melody notes are on the guitar, you should play it with the *index finger* and not with the thumb as in the previous chapters. This is quite important and even though it may feel clumsy at first, you will quickly get accustomed to it.

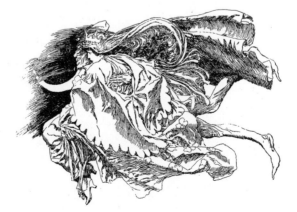

Tom Dooley - Melody

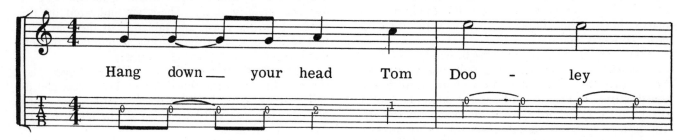

Hang down your head Tom Doo - ley

Hang down your head and cry. Hang down your head Tom

Doo - ley, Poor boy you're bound to die.

Let us now look at the solo version of *Tom Dooley* in the fingerpicking style. As usual, look first at the rhythmic patterns involved in this song. You will notice that only quarter notes are used. Rhythmically this makes things rather simple: 1, 2, 3, 4, with no eighth notes to worry about.

The work to be done by the right hand is not difficult; pinches and thumb notes are all that is required. Notice that the thumb alternately plays the fifth and fourth strings in the C chord and the sixth and fourth strings in the G7 chord. This is called *alternating bass.* The notes which the thumb plays for the alternating bass in any particular chord should be thoroughly learned. It is most important that the thumb consistently play the correct notes.

The whole song only requires two chords for the left hand: C and G7. There are, however, many notes out of the chords. Be aware of the large amount of motion required of the left hand. It is typical of fingerpicking.

The best way to learn a fingerpicking song is the following:

STEP ONE: Holding the chords indicated in the music, use the index finger of the right hand to *pick out the melody notes.* These are indicated by the letter "I" in the music and tablature of the solo. This will accustom you to the motions required of the left hand to get the *out of the chord* notes.

STEP TWO: Without using the index finger, play the bass line with the thumb using the correct chords and making sure that the correct strings are being played. Thus you will be playing all the notes marked "T" in the tablature.

STEP THREE: Put the two parts together by using both the index finger and the thumb, playing both pinches and thumb notes. Make sure the correct bass strings are being played and the melody corresponds to the proper bass note. The CHORD ANALYSIS BOX will be of assistance in the first measure. After learning this, the rest of the song should present little difficulty.

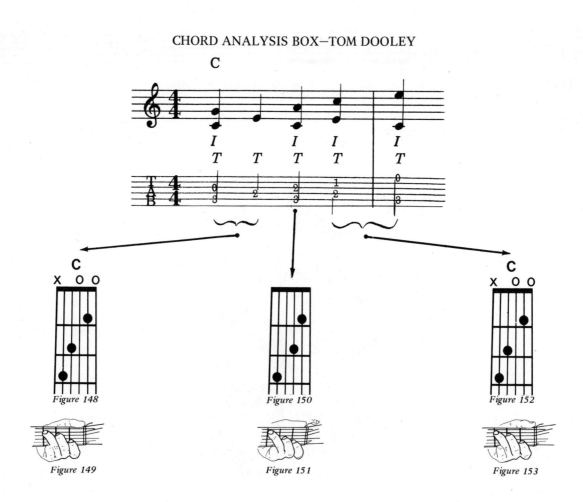

CHORD ANALYSIS BOX—TOM DOOLEY

Figure 148

Figure 149

Figure 150

Figure 151

Figure 152

Figure 153

Tom Dooley - Solo

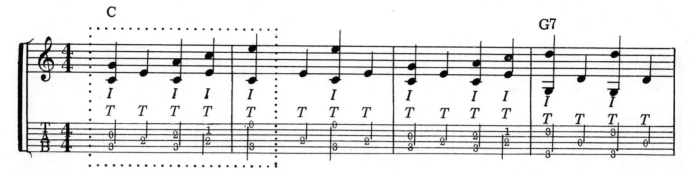

GO TELL AUNT RHODY — FINGERPICKING SOLO

Again you have an opportunity to compare the Carter style solo of Chapter 2 with the fingerpicking version given here. Learn the melody on the treble strings first and then learn the fingerpicking version.

Go Tell Aunt Rhody - Melody

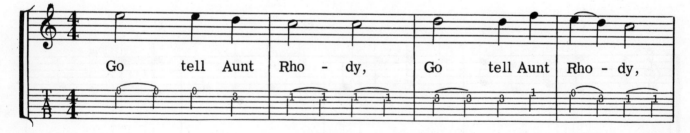

Go tell Aunt Rho - dy, Go tell Aunt Rho - dy,

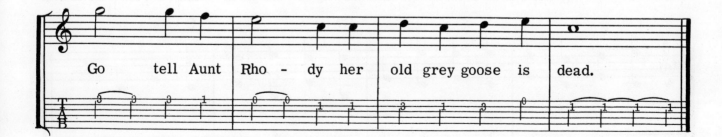

Go tell Aunt Rho - dy her old grey goose is dead.

Go Tell Aunt Rhody - Solo

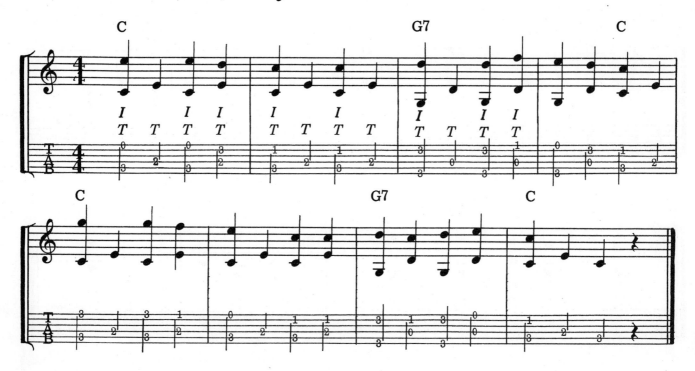

MARY HAD A LITTLE LAMB

Nursery rhymes can be a lot of fun. If you have some friends who can fingerpick, try this song as a round.

Mary Had A Little Lamb - Solo

This slow song should give you ample practice in accuracy in fingerpicking.

Hush, Little Baby - Melody

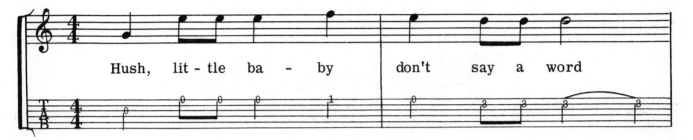

C   G7
Hush, little baby don't say a word,

                                  C
Poppa's gonna buy you a mocking bird.

And if that mocking bird don't sing,
Poppa's gonna buy you a diamond ring.

And if that diamond ring turns brass,
Poppa's gonna buy you a looking glass.

And if that looking glass is broke,
Poppa's gonna buy you a billy goat.

And if that billy goat don't pull,
Poppa's gonna buy you a cart and bull.

And if that cart and bull turn over,
Poppa's gonna buy you a dog named Rover.

And if that dog named Rover won't bark,
Poppa's gonna buy you a horse and cart.

And if that horse and cart fall down,
You're still the sweetest little baby in town.

Hush, Little Baby - Solo

YANKEE DOODLE – CHORD CHANGES

This song makes extensive use of the G7 chord position for playing notes which are out of the chord on the top three strings of the guitar as illustrated in the CHORD ANALYSIS BOX. Make sure the chord changes from C to G7 are smooth before going on to the next song. The *out of the chord* note in the next to the last measure is obtained by moving the middle finger from the fifth string to the third string at the second fret as shown in Figures 163 and 165.

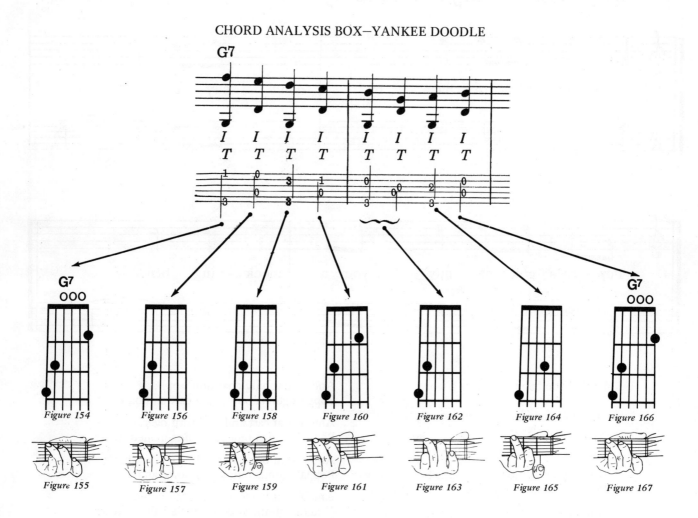

CHORD ANALYSIS BOX—YANKEE DOODLE

Figure 154   Figure 156   Figure 158   Figure 160   Figure 162   Figure 164   Figure 166

Figure 155   Figure 157   Figure 159   Figure 161   Figure 163   Figure 165   Figure 167

Yankee Doodle - Solo

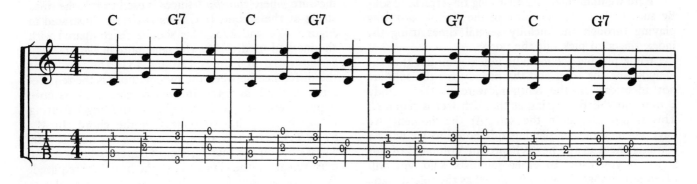

Here we undertake our first long fingerpicking solo. Be sure to learn the position of the melody notes by playing through the melody several times using the index finger to pick out the notes.

While playing the melody, you may notice that the melody for the song and the melody for the solo are not identical. In the tenth measure of the melody a note on the first string at the fifth fret is required. This is not played in the solo. At the moment, we have no methods of playing this note but we will be learning them in the next chapter in Volume 2 of this series. If you listen to other guitarists' solo, you will often notice that the melody played as the solo departs from the melody of the song as sung. These departures reflect the guitarist's style and feeling for arrangement.

The most difficult portion of the solo is the third measure where the *third* finger is used to fret the third string at the second fret. This is clearly illustrated in Figures 174 and 175. This should be compared with the method used to fret the same note in *Tom Dooley* as illustrated in Figures 150 and 151. The reason for the difference between the two methods is the requirement of the bass notes. In *Tom Dooley* the bass note required was on the fifth string so the finger fretting the fifth string has to remain in the chord. In *My Home's Across the Smokey Mountains* the note is with a bass note on the fourth string. Thus the second finger must remain in the chord to fret the bass note required. The requirements for the bass notes will often determine which fingers are used to fret *out of the chord* notes in fingerpicking.

My Home's Across The Smokey Mountains - Melody

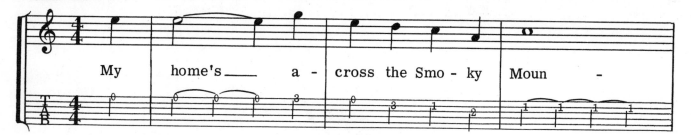

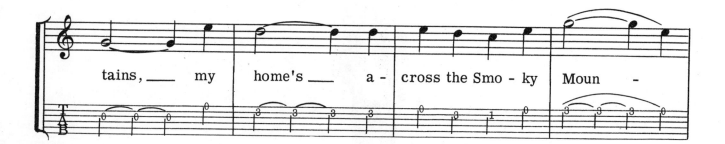

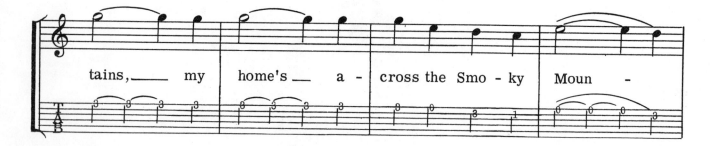

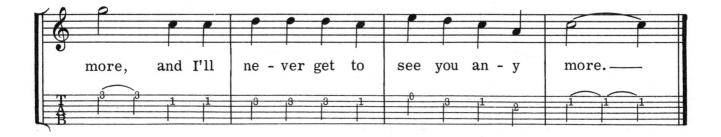

C
My home's across the Smokey Mountains,
  G7   C
My home's across the Smokey Mountains,

My home's across the Smokey Mountains,
      G7   C
And I'll never get to see you any more, more, more,
      G7
And I'll never get to see you any more.

I'm leavin' on a Monday mornin' (3)
And I'll never get to see you any more, more, more,
And I'll never get to see you any more.

Rock my baby, feed her candy, (3)
And I'll never get to see her any more, more, more,
And I'll never get to see her any more.

Where's that silver ring I gave you? (3)
And I'll never get to see you any more, more, more,
And I'll never get to see you any more.

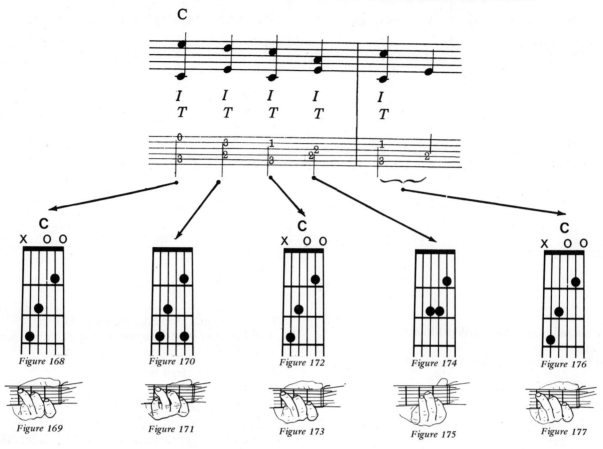

Figure 168   Figure 170   Figure 172   Figure 174   Figure 176

Figure 169   Figure 171   Figure 173   Figure 175   Figure 177

My Home's Across The Smokey Mountains - Solo

WORRIED MAN BLUES —
FINGERPICKING F CHORDS

In the fifth measure of the solo of this song we will use an F chord. All F chords in fingerpicking must have the sixth string fretted at the first fret. See the discussion of the F chord in *Wabash Cannon Ball* and Figures 178 and 179. This is necessary since the bass line in the F chord alternates from the sixth string to the fourth string. The first encounter with the F chord has been detailed in the CHORD ANALYSIS BOX.

It should be noticed that in the eighth measure, the bass line has been changed slightly. When not much picking is going on and we are playing a C chord, we can use a simple trick to add some interest to the fingerpicking. The third beat of the measure can be played on the third fret of the *sixth* string instead of the fifth string. This is done by simply moving the third finger over a string. Don't forget to move it back before beginning the next measure. This pattern is sometimes called a "walking bass."

Worried Man Blues - Melody

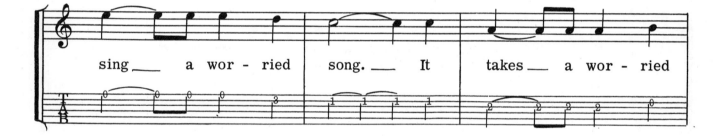

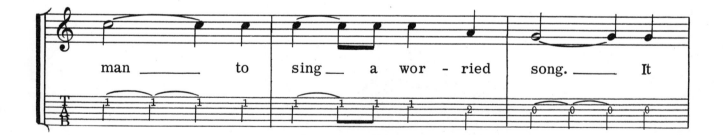

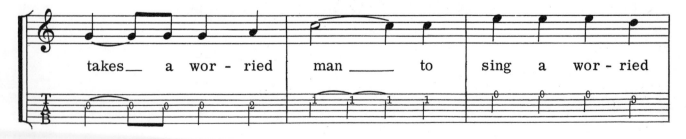

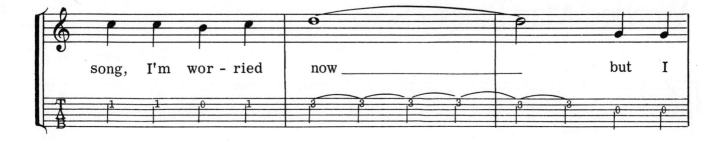

song, I'm wor - ried now _____ but I

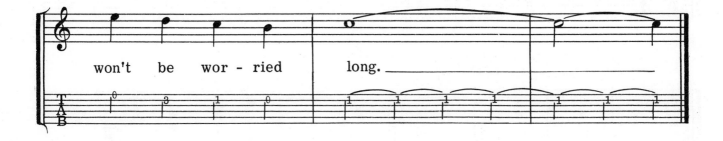

won't be wor - ried long. _____

CHORD ANALYSIS BOX—WORRIED MAN BLUES

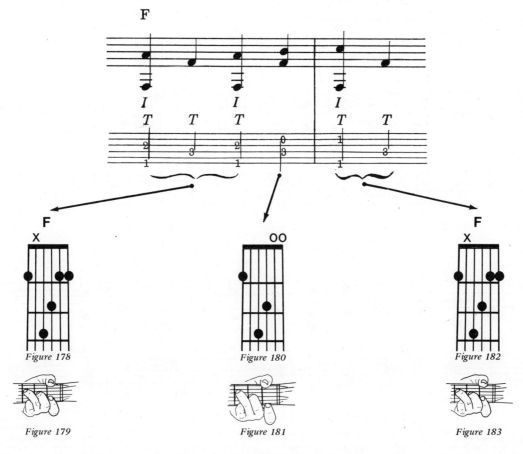

Figure 178

Figure 179

Figure 180

Figure 181

Figure 182

Figure 183

Worried Man Blues - Solo

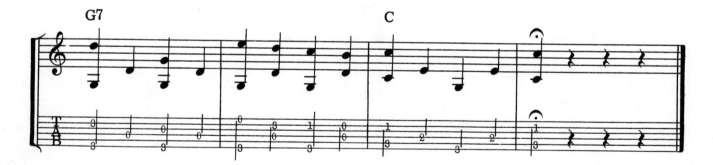

In this song we find additional examples of the use of the walking bass pattern in measures four and sixteen.

The F chord required at the beginning of the twelfth measure is slightly more difficult since one must fret the first string at the third fret with the little finger as shown in Figures 190 and 191. However, in the next beat one returns to the normal F chord (Figures 192 and 193).

Red River Valley - Melody

C
From this valley they say you are going,

G7
I will miss your bright eyes and sweet smile,

C   F
For they say you are taking the sunshine

C   G7   C
That has brightened our pathways a while.

Oh just think of the valley you're leaving,
How lonely and said it will be.
And just think of the true heart you're breaking
And the grief you are causing to me.

Come and sit by my side if you love me,
Do not hasten to bid me adieu;
But remember the Red River Valley
And the cowboy who loved you so true.

CHORD ANALYSIS BOX—RED RIVER VALLEY

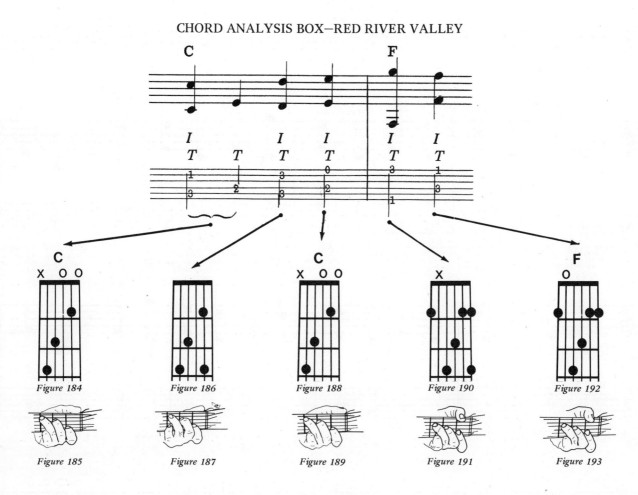

Figure 184   Figure 186   Figure 188   Figure 190   Figure 192

Figure 185   Figure 187   Figure 189   Figure 191   Figure 193

Red River Valley - Solo

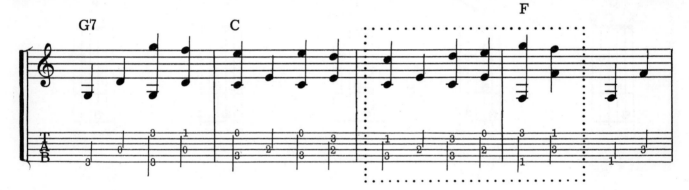

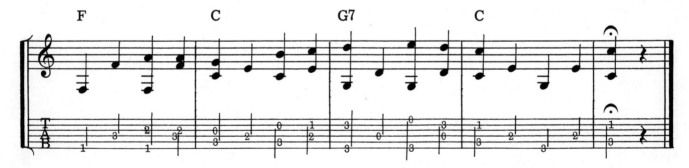

GO TELL AUNT RHODY — OFF-BEATS

We are now going to learn to fingerpick melodies on the off-beats which will provide us with much more rhythmic freedom in our fingerpicking solos. This is one of the few places in this book where we will have to resort to exercises instead of illustrative examples. I hope the student will not skip them.

First, what is an "off-beat"? Review the exercises in Chapter 2 on the double brush. You will recall that an off-beat is a note that comes between the beats of the measure. In a measure of $\frac{4}{4}$ time, the beats are counted 1, 2, 3, 4, and any note that is counted "&" is an off-beat. The notes corresponding to the numbers are "on-beats." In Carter picking, all the off-beats were the second brush of the double brush or the index

finger picking a note after a thumb note as in *Wildwood Flower*. We shall now extend this latter technique to fingerpicking.

The off-beats we will now be playing will be played with the index finger. You will have noticed that all of the melody notes that we have played up to this point in our study of fingerpicking have been played synchronously with the thumb—they have all been on-beats. We will now play notes between the thumb beats—off-beats. Before we get into the song itself, let's work on some isolated examples of off-beats. For each of the ten measures below, fill in the count and how the measure should be played in the fingerpicking style.

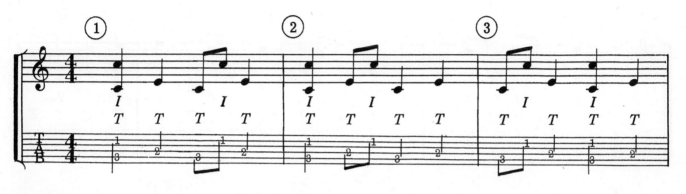

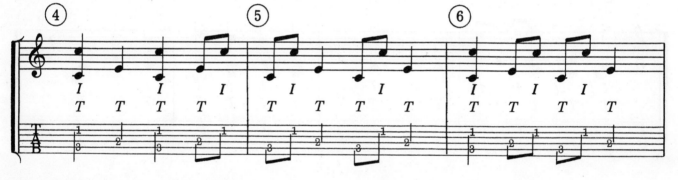

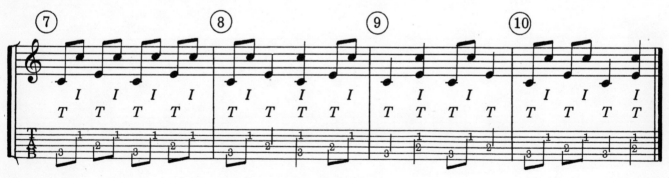

1—1, 2, 3, &, 4. Pinch, Thumb, Thumb-Index, Thumb.
2—1, 2, &, 3, 4. Pinch, Thumb-Index, Thumb, Thumb.
3—1, &, 2, 3, 4. _____
4—_____
5—_____ Thumb-Index, Thumb, Thumb-Index,
       Thumb.
6—_____
7—1, &, 2, &, 3, &, 4, &. _____
       _____
8—_____
9—_____

10—_____

Now play the example measures until the rhythm is smooth. Try putting together combinations of two or three measures to check your smoothness and understanding of the techniques of off-beats.

Try to identify the off-beat patterns in *Go Tell Aunt Rhody* with those in the exercises above. Also compare this version with off-beats to the previous version without off-beats.

Go Tell Aunt Rhody - Solo

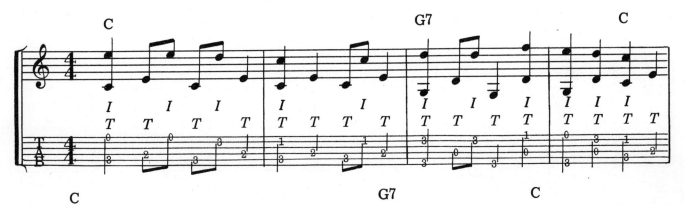

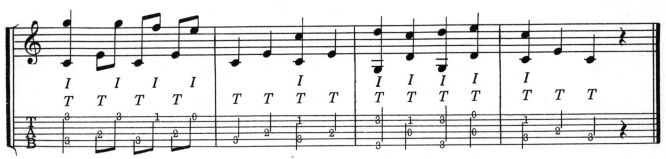

In this song again compare the off-beats with those given in the exercises for *Go Tell Aunt Rhody.* Make sure the placement of the off-beat is correct. Clap the rhythm and then play it on the guitar.

Worried Man Blues - Solo

Again we have the opportunity to compare two versions of the same song, one with off-beats and one without.

Red River Valley - Solo

If you compare the notes played by the index finger in the solo and the melody of this song, you will find that many notes in the guitar solo have no counterpart in the melody. Similarly, there is a note in the melody that is not played in the guitar solo.

The purpose of adding notes in the guitar solo which do not appear in the melody is to fill in long spaces where no melody notes occur. Examples of such places are in the fourth, fifth, eighth and ninth measures of the melody. Here one melody note is held for six beats. This means that if we were to play only the melody notes, nothing would be played for those six beats. Instead we insert notes to fill in the space with interesting fingerpicking material. Only experience will determine which notes can be inserted without destroying the feeling of the song.

Hard, Ain't It Hard - Melody

C   F
It's hard, ain't it hard, ain't it hard,
C   G7
To love one who never will love you.
C   F
It's hard and it's hard, ain't it hard, great God,
C   G7   C
To love one who never will be true.

There is a place in this old town,
And that's where my true love lays around.
And she sits upon those other men's knees,
And tells them what she never would tell me.

Don't go there to drink and gamble,
Don't go there your sorrows for to drown.
That hard likker place is a low-down disgrace,
It's the meanest damn place in this town.

The first time I saw my true love,
She was standin' by the door.
And the last time I saw her false-hearted face,
She was dead on that bar-room floor.

Hard, Ain't It Hard - Solo

MY HOME'S ACROSS THE SMOKEY MOUNTAINS

To finish off, here's a little piece of homework.
If you feel up to it, you can finish this song with off-
beats wherever you like . . . good luck.

My Home's Across The Smokey Mountains - Solo

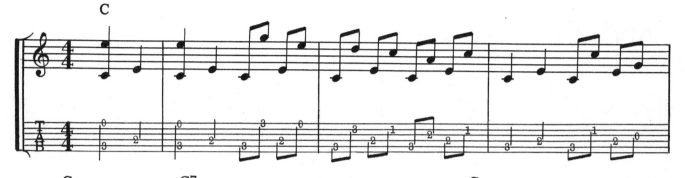

DOING IT ALL BY YOURSELF

In this chapter we have the melodies of several songs that you should arrange for yourself in the styles we have been studying in this book. The songs with the tablature writing in the bass portion of the guitar should be arranged in the Carter style and the songs with the tab in the upper registers should be fingerpicked.

Remember that there is no one right way to arrange a song. Every creative guitarist should be able to produce at least five or six arrangements of each song in this chapter. This will be the real test to see how well you have learned the basics of instrumental folk guitar in this book.

Abdullah Abulbul Amir

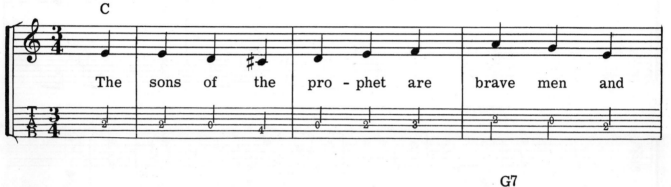

The sons of the pro - phet are brave men and

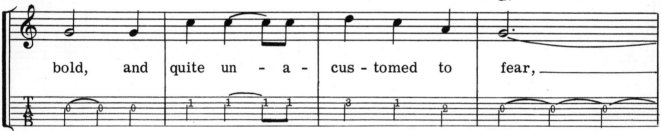

bold, and quite un - a - cus - tomed to fear,

But the bra - vest of all was a man, I am

told named Ab - dul - lah Bul - bul A - mir.

When they needed a man to encourage the van,
Or to harass a foe from the rear,
Storm fort or redoubt, they had only to shout
For Abdullah Abulbul Amir.

This son of the desert in battle aroused,
Could spit twenty men on his spear.

A terrible creature when sober or soused,
Was Abdullah Abulbul Amir.

Now the heroes were plenty and well known to fame
Who fought in the ranks of the Czar;
But the bravest of these was a man by the name
of Ian Skavinsky Skivar.

Billy Boy

Oh,— where have you been, Bil-ly boy Bil-ly Boy? Oh,—
where have you been, charm-in' Bil-ly,——— I have
been to seek a wife, she's the i-dol of my life, She's— a
young thing, and can-not leave her mo-ther.———

Where does she live, Billy boy, etc.
She lives on the hill, forty miles from the mill.

Did she bid you to come in?
Yes, she bade me to come in, and to kiss her on the chin.

Did she take your hat?
Yes, she took my hat, and she threw it at the cat.

Did she set for you a chair?
Yes, she set for me a chair, but the bottom wasn't there.

Buffalo Gals

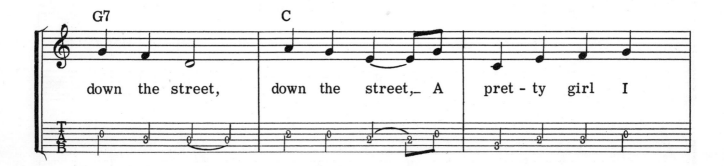

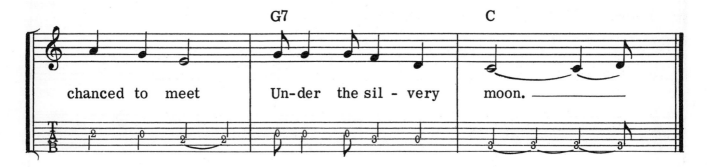

CHORUS:

Buffalo gals won't you come out tonight,
Come out tonight, come out tonight.
Buffalo gals won't you come out tonight,
And dance by the light of the moon.

I asked her if she'd stop and talk,
Stop and talk, stop and talk,
Her feet covered up the whole sidewalk,
She was fair to view.

I asked her if she'd be my wife,
Be my wife, be my wife,
Then I'd be happy all my life,
If she'd marry me.

Camptown Races

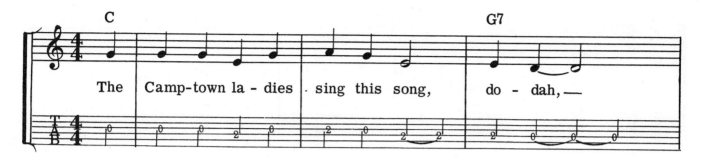

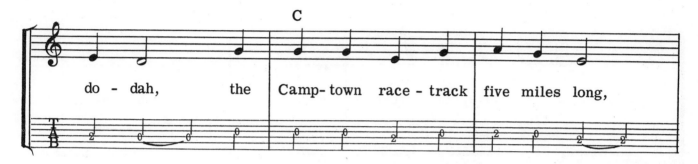

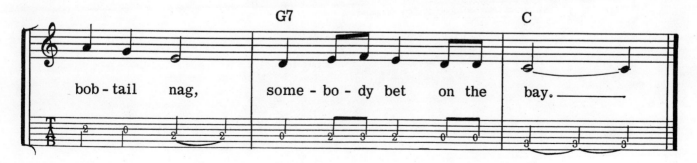

Careless Love

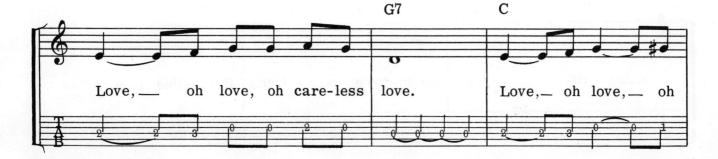

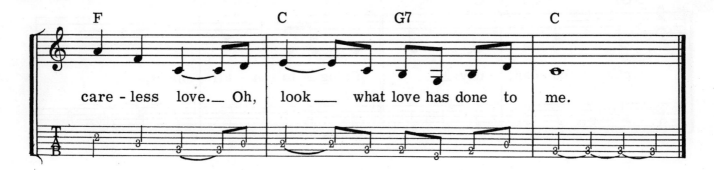

Once my apron strings were long,
And then you passed by with a song.

Now my apron strings won't tie,
You pass my open door right by.

Clementine

In a cav - ern, in a can - yon, ex - ca-

va - ting for a mine, Dwelt a mi - ner, for - ty

ni - ner, and his daugh - ter Clem - en - tine.

Cumberland Gap

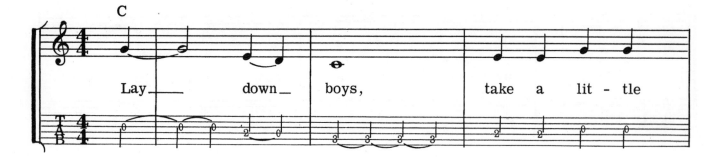

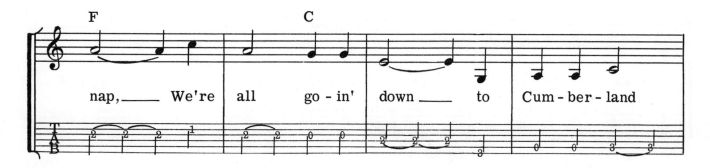

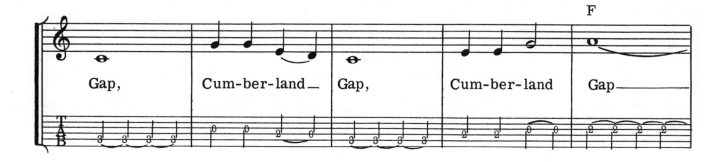

Darling Corey

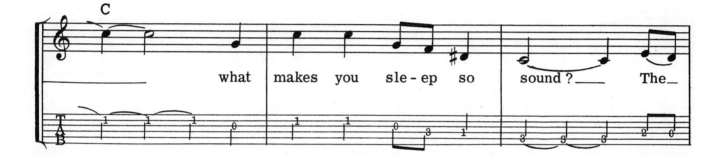

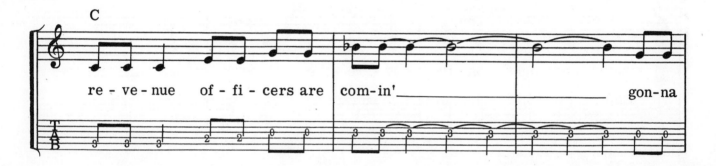

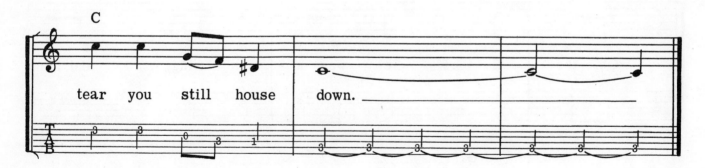

127

E-ri-e Canal

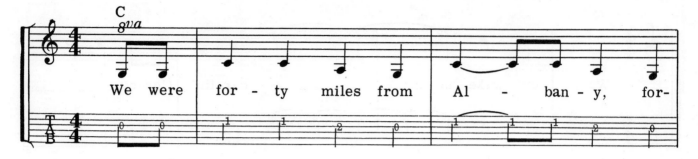

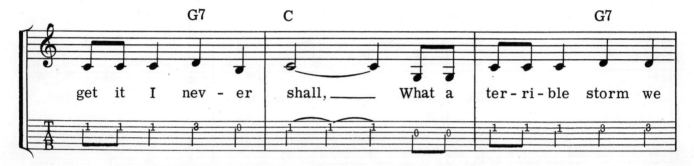

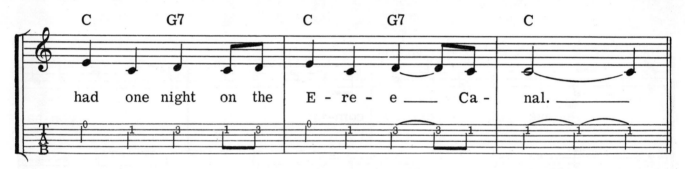

Chorus

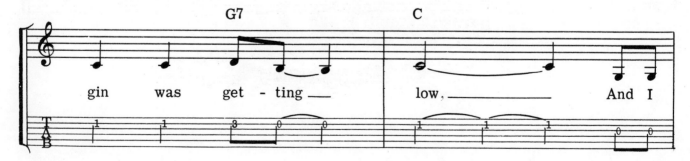

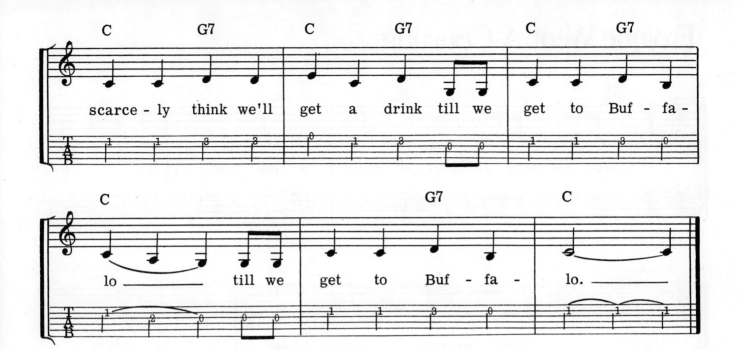

scarce - ly think we'll | get a drink till we | get to Buf - fa -

lo _____ till we | get to Buf - fa - | lo. _____

We were loaded down with barley,
We were chuck up full of rye,
And the captain, he looked down at me
With his goddam wicked eye.

Our captain, he came up on deck,
With a spy glass in his hand,
And the fog it was so darned thick
That he could not spy the land.

Our cook, she was a grand old gal,
She had a ragged dress,
We hoisted her upon the pole,
As a signal of distress.

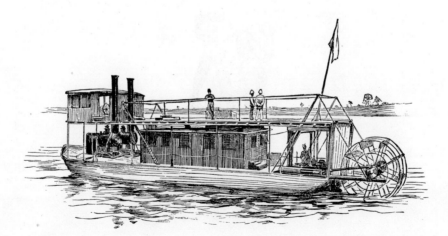

Froggie Went A-Courting

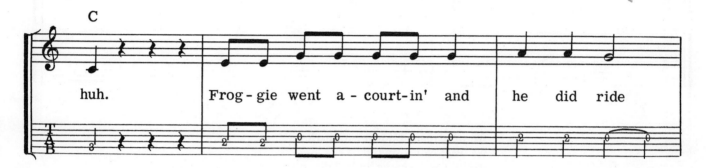

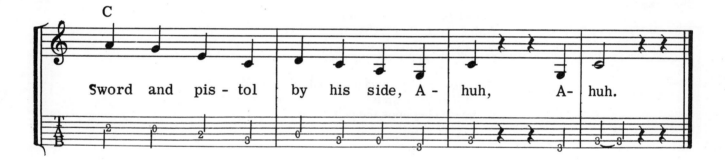

Handsome Molly

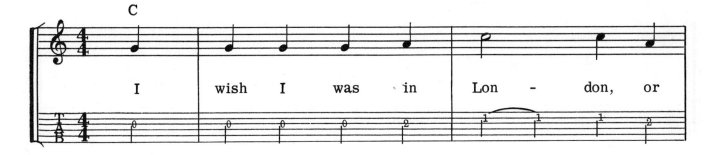

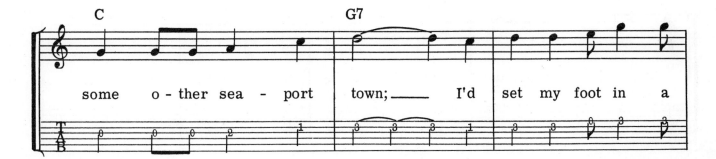

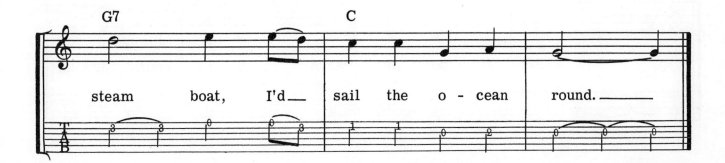

While sailing around the ocean,
While sailing 'round the sea,
I'd think of handsome Molly
Wherever she may be.

You rode to church last Sunday
You passed me on by;
I know your mind is changin'
By the rovin' of your eye.

Don't you remember, Molly,
When you gave me your right hand?
Said if you ever married,
Then I would be the man.

Now you've broke your promise Molly,
Go home with whom you please,
While my poor heart is breakin'
You're lying at your ease.

Her hair was black as a raven,
Her eyes as black as coal,
Her cheeks was like lilies
Out in the morning cold.

Home On The Range

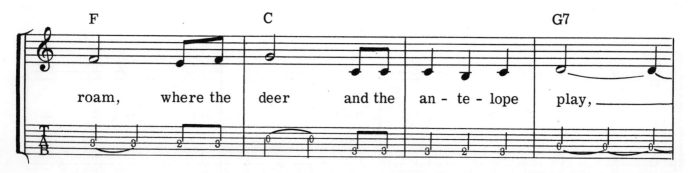

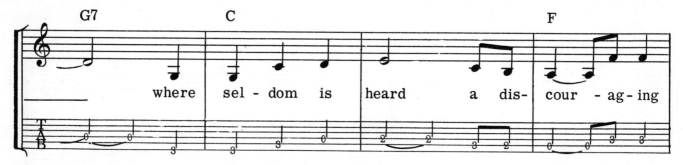

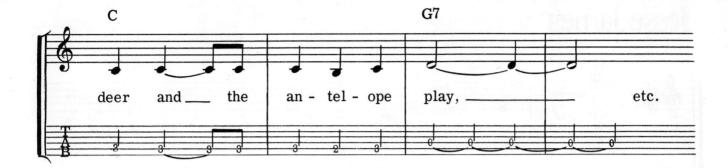

deer   and ___   the   an - tel - ope   play, _____   etc.

Jesse James

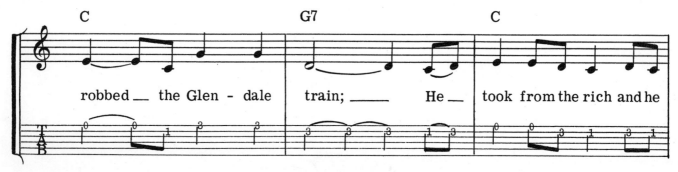

Chorus

Old Time Religion

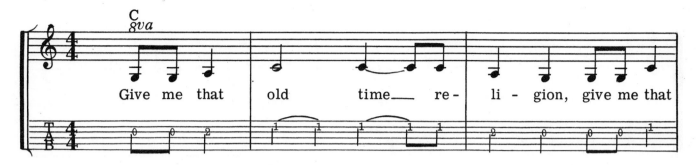

John Brown's Body

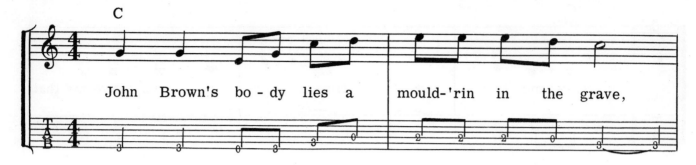

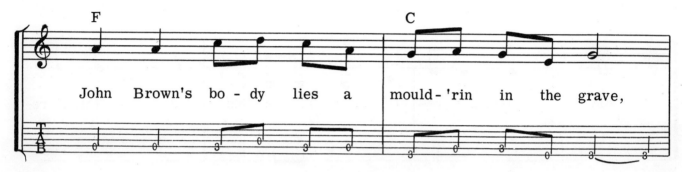

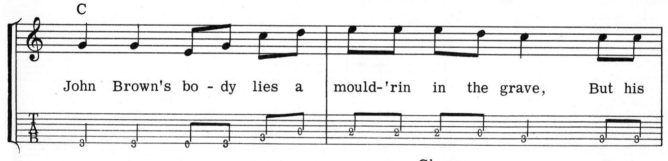

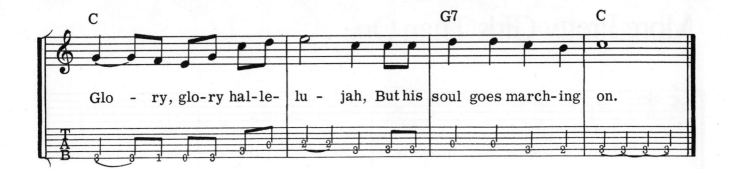

Glo - ry, glo-ry hal-le- lu - jah, But his soul goes march-ing on.

More Pretty Girls Than One

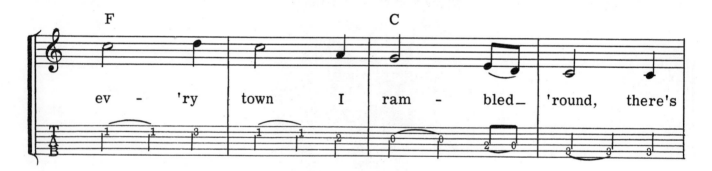

Stagolee

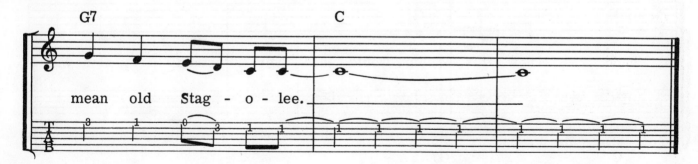

The Ship Titanic

Oh,__ they built the ship Titanic, to sail the ocean

blue, and they thought they had a ship that__ the

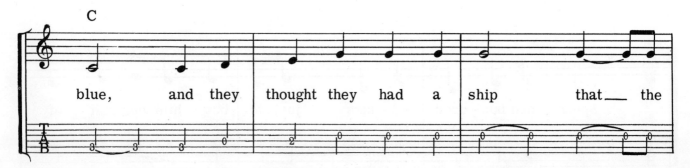

wa - ter would ne - ver leak through, But __ the Lord's al-might - y

hand knew this ship would ne - ver stand; it was

sad__ when the great__ ship went down. _____

Oh, they sailed from the coast of England,
And were almost on the shore,
When the rich refused
To associate with the poor,
So they put them down below,
Where they were the first to go;
It was sad when the great ship went down.

The boat was full of sin,
And the sides were 'bout to bust,
When the captain he shouted,
"Women and children first."
Oh, the captain tried to wire,
But the wires were all on fire;
It was sad when the great ship went down.

Oh, they swung the lifeboats out
O're a dark and stormy sea,
When the band struck up with,
"Nearer My God to Thee."
Little children wept and cried,
As the waves swept o'er the side;
It was sad when the great ship went down.

Study War No More

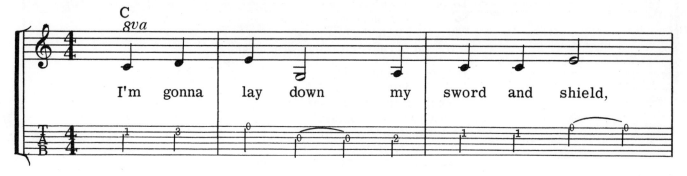

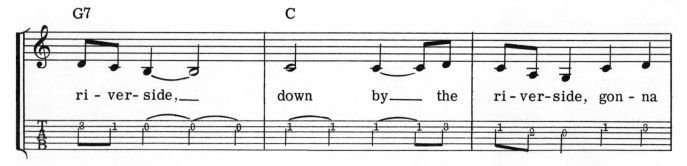

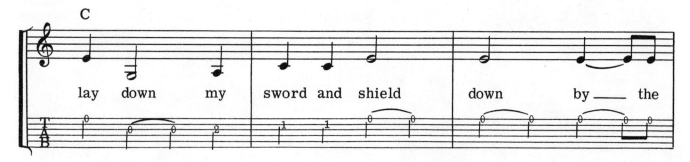

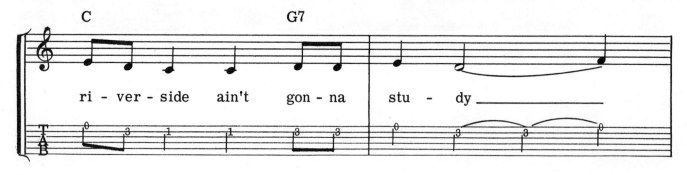

war   no   more.

Streets of Laredo

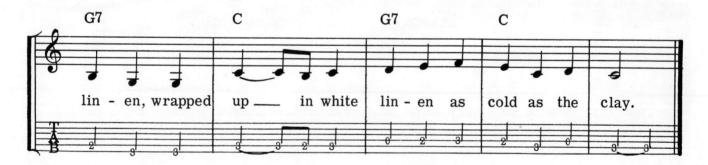

Swanee River

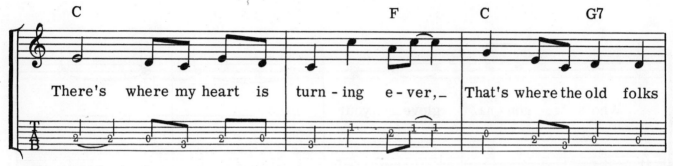

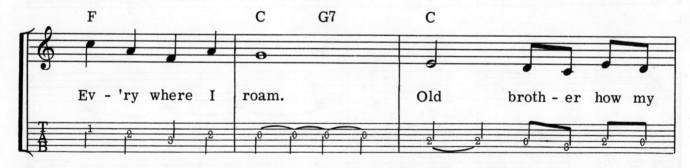

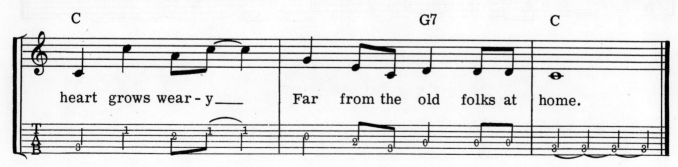

Who's Gonna Shoe Your Pretty Little Foot?

Who's gon-na shoe your pret-ty lit-tle foot?____

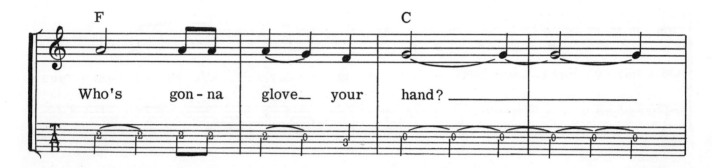

Who's gon-na glove___ your hand? _____

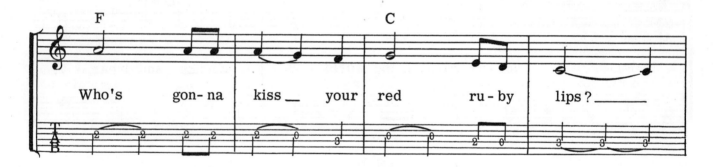

Who's gon-na kiss___ your red ru-by lips?_____

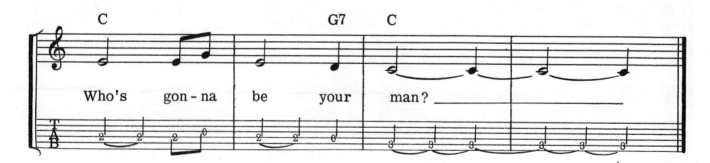

Who's gon-na be your man? _____

APPENDIX A - TUNING THE GUITAR

Putting a guitar into good tune is, perhaps, one of the more challenging aspects of guitar playing. It does not require an exceptionally "good ear," nor does it require perfect pitch. It does, however, require practice and, in the beginning, it requires someone to tell you when your guitar is in tune when you are not sure. Below several methods of tuning the guitar will be described. The student should try each one and find the easiest method for him.

Tuning the guitar can be conveniently divided into two parts. The first part consists of getting one string of the guitar "in tune" or deciding that a string is in tune. The second part of tuning puts the other strings into relative tune with the one string.

ABSOLUTE PITCH DETERMINATION

We must first get one string into tune. There are several methods for doing this, some arbitrary and some precise.

Kentucky Windage

This method is only good when you are playing by yourself because there is absolutely no way one can get in tune with anyone else by this method. It is handy when you have no way of determining the absolute pitch of any note on the guitar.

The method consists of tuning the sixth string, the lowest pitched, from a completely slack condition until it doesn't buzz by slowly increasing the tension on the string. Start with the sixth string loosened until it resembles a thick rubber band. Then, while sounding it, slowly increase the tension. At some point it should stop buzzing against the frets. You can stop at this point or increase the tension slightly depending on how low a note is produced. This string is now considered to be the reference pitch for tuning the rest of the strings—it has arbitrarily been called "in tune." You can now go to the section called Relative Pitch Determination.

Tuning Forks

The most accurate (and inexpensive) device for determining the absolute pitch of a note is a tuning fork. They commonly come in two pitches, A and Bb. The A (440) is handier for the guitar player while the Bb is used in orchestras for tuning. The tines (the long, rod-shaped projections) are manufactured so that when they are gently squeezed and suddenly released, they will vibrate at exactly 440 vibrations per second; the tone produced in this way corresponds exactly to the pitch of an A note.

The tuning fork should never be hit against any hard object nor should it be struck with anything but a special soft rubber hammer. The best way of sounding the tuning fork is to squeeze the tines between your fingers and then let your fingers slip off the fork. This will produce a tone of moderate intensity without

danger of injuring the tuning fork (and thus changing its pitch).

To amplify the sound of the tuning fork, hold the base of the fork against the top of the guitar or against the bridge. This will make the sound louder and tuning easier.

Using the A (440) tuning fork, you can tune the fifth string open, or the third string at the second fret, or the first string at the fifth fret to the pitch of the tuning fork, A. However, the fifth string open will be two octaves below the pitch of the fork and the third string at the second fret will be one octave below. Thus, it may be easiest for the beginner to tune the first string at the fifth fret to the pitch of the tuning fork. Once this is done you can go to the section on Relative Pitch Determination.

Pitch Pipes

Pitch pipes are small reeds encased in plastic or metal. They are adjusted so that when they are set in motion by gently blowing into the pipe, they will vibrate to produce a definite tone. The pitch of most pitch pipes can vary with how hard they are blown. This is worse with some pitch pipes than with others. They come either in single pipes or in groups corresponding to the open strings of the guitar or to the full chromatic scale of 12 notes. With the single pipes, be sure to select one that corresponds to the pitch of the guitar strings: E, A, D, G, or B. The higher range pitch pipes are usually easier to use. The use is similar to that described for the tuning fork.

The multiple pipes or the chromatic pitch pipes are used in a similar way but one must select the pipe corresponding to the string that is to be tuned.

The most attractive of the pitch pipes is the multiple pipes with one pipe corresponding to each string of the guitar. Somehow, guitars tuned to these pitch pipes are seldom in tune and will need further adjustment by other methods.

Miscellaneous Methods

Several electronic instruments are on the market but these are usually very expensive. For this reason they will not be discussed here; they usually come with extensive instructions.

In some parts of the country, the dial tone on the telephone corresponds to Bb (fifth string at the first fret, third string at the third fret). This is often very useful, and quite inexpensive.

After one string has either been put into tune or has been designated as "in tune" the other strings of the guitar must be brought into tune relative to the "correct" string. This is discussed below in the section called Relative Pitch Determination.

RELATIVE PITCH DETERMINATION

The strings of the guitar are tuned from the bass string to the treble string, E, A, D, G, B, E. It can be easily shown that when the sixth string is fretted at the fifth fret it should produce the same tone as the fifth string open. The sixth string fretted at the fifth fret will sound an A note which corresponds to the A note played on the fifth string open. If the guitar is not in tune, the two notes will *not* have the same pitch. Tuning consists of adjusting one of the strings until the same tone *is* produced.

Let us assume that the sixth string is at the correct pitch. (One must always start by assuming that at least one string is correct. This is done by the various methods described above.) We now fret the sixth string at the fifth fret and adjust the fifth string so that it is at the same pitch. Sound the sixth string at the fifth fret, wait a few seconds, then sound the fifth string open. Before touching the tuning machines, decide in your mind whether the fifth string is too high (sharp) or too low (flat). If it is flat, simply tune it up by increasing the tension on it until it sounds right. Then repeat the whole procedure until you are very sure that the pitch of the two notes is identical. If the fifth string is sharp, lower the string until the pitch is the same. However, with many guitars it is better to lower a sharp string past the correct pitch until it is flat and then to bring the string up to the correct pitch. In this way the strings do not slip after tuning and the guitar will stay in tune longer.

The procedure is continued to the other strings in the following way. The fifth string fretted at the fifth fret is matched to the fourth string open. Then the fourth string at the fifth fret is matched to the third string open. However, the third string at the *fourth fret* (not the fifth fret) is matched to the second string open and finally the second string at the fifth fret is used to tune the first string open. This procedure is summarized in the tuning diagram in Figure 194.

Figure 194

A similar procedure can be followed if a string other than the sixth string has been put into absolute tune. For instance, if a pitch pipe was used to tune the third string at the second fret to A, we can now use the third string to ·tune all the other strings. The third string at the fourth fret can be used to tune the second string open. The second string open is then matched by adjusting the first string open. The fourth string at the fifth fret is tuned to match the third string open and the sixth string at the fifth fret is then tuned to match the fifth string open. A similar method can be easily developed using any string as a starting point and the frets indicated in Figure 194.

After the tuning by frets has been completed, the procedure should be repeated to check the tuning of all the strings. Minor adjustments will usually be necessary the second time around to achieve good tuning.

By very gently touching (not fretting) strings in certain positions, various overtones can be produced. These overtones can be used for tuning the guitar. The principles behind the production of these overtones, called harmonics, is explained in any text book on elementary physics and will not be discussed here.

The first step is to learn how to play the harmonics. The easiest harmonic to play is the one produced at the twelfth fret of the sixth string. Fret the sixth string at the twelfth fret; now let up on the string with the left hand until the finger is just barely touching the string. Sound the string close to the bridge—you should get a very "pure" sounding tone which should correspond to the pitch of the fourth string at the second fret. With a little practice you should be able to play the harmonics.

The harmonics used in tuning are those that correspond to the fifth and seventh frets. The harmonic on the sixth string at the fifth fret should be the same pitch as the harmonic on the fifth string at the seventh fret. Notice that the harmonic continues to sound long after you have removed the "fretting" finger. This makes it very easy to tune by harmonics. The harmonic of the fifth string at the fifth fret corresponds to the fourth string at the seventh fret. The fourth string at the fifth fret corresponds to the third string at the seventh fret. These harmonic relations are summarized in Figure 195, below.

A slightly different method is used for tuning the first and second strings. The harmonic at the sixth string, fifth fret corresponds to the first string *open*. The harmonic on the seventh fret of the sixth string corresponds to the pitch of the second string *open*. These relations are summarized in Figure 196.

Figure 195   *Figure 196*